I Came, I Saw, and I'm Still Here

Written by Timesha G. Mohan

PublishAmerica
Baltimore

First printing

PublishAmerica has allowed this work to remain exactly as the author intended, verbatim, without editorial input.

ISBN: 978-1-60836-273-8
PUBLISHED BY PUBLISHAMERICA, LLLP
www.publishamerica.com
Baltimore

Printed in the United States of America

In Memory Of
Glenn Schultz
Ronald Mullins
Elizabeth Rolland
Elaine Hill
Ernest James Rolland Jr.
Oscar Hill

Preface

When I think of an author, someone who writes a book, the first thing that comes to mind is someone in their late thirties or early forties, someone who has gone from infant, to toddler, to adolescent, to adult, to mother or father, or even grandparents. Someone who has obliviously lived a great deal of life as well as some one who would have great stories to tell. I've said to myself numerous of times "I'm only nineteen years old, my life hasn't even begun". That's when the most inspirational person in my life, my mom, my mentor, my everything, told me "Timesha, the one thing that you fail to realize is that you've gone through more things at the age of nineteen, than most people have gone through in their entire lives". That's when I decided that I would write this book. The idea that my book might never be published didn't even bother me at all. I knew that this was something that I had to do. I figured that writing a book about the ups and downs that I've been through was my very own special way of getting some kind of closure.

Contents

I Came, I Saw,
and I'm Still Here

Chapter 1
Doomed from the Beginning

Some people might say that I was doomed from the beginning, a bastard, born out of wedlock. To be exact, March 4, 1985 at 8:24pm was the day that I entered this world as Timesha Ge'na Mullins. The daughter of Katherine Williams and Kevin Mullins, of whom we'll refer to as "Egg" and "Sperm" because they sure as hell don't deserve to be called mom and dad. I was born in Chicago, IL at Mary Thompson Hospital. Both Egg and Sperm were twenty-two years old and not married. I was the first child for both of them; Although, I've been told that Egg had a miscarriage with a baby boy in 1984. Both good and bad, otherwise I wouldn't exist. Egg was one of three children and her parents were never married. Sperm was one of four children, his parents were married, but his mother would later die shortly after giving birth to her last child.

It's kind of a funny story the way they met each other. Egg's mother (Grandma Yolanda) was having problems with her car and was referred to Barry's Auto Body Shop. Barry's Auto Body Shop was located on the west side of Chicago and owned by a local mechanic named Barry Mullins Sr., who was also the father of Sperm. Grandma Yolanda and Grandpa Barry became friends. As time passed, Grandma Yolanda soon began to baby-sit Grandpa Barry's youngest son, Donald. Donald took a liking to Egg and told her that he had an older brother name Kevin who drove a Cadillac and he wanted her to meet him. Once, Egg & Sperm met, they fell head over heels for each other and then I was conceived. Grandpa Barry owned a two-story house on the west side of Chicago, which is were I lived the first three years of my life with Egg and Sperm. Although, they were madly in love with each other, we all know that nothing lasts forever. Both Egg and Sperm chose to go their separate ways in 1988.

My earliest childhood memories begin at the age of four. I remember that Egg and Sperm had separated and Egg and I moved into an apartment in Forest Park, IL, while Sperm stayed in Chicago. I can honestly say that at the age of four I was happy. I was an only child, but you would never guess that with all the toys that I had lying around the house. Fisher Price kitchen set, stuffed animals, jack-in-a-box, My Little Pony, Barbie dolls, Cabbage Patch Kids, Care Bears, you name it, I had it. My earliest memories were mostly of toys, but I also remember that Egg worked for Jay's Potato Chips, so you can imagine how much junk food I ate. These were all good memories, but they would soon come to a halt.

I attended pre-school in Forest Park, IL, and I remember that I wet my pants one day in school while playing on the monkey bars. The school called Egg but she was at work. This particular day Egg's older sister, Auntie Sherry, was in town and staying at our house. Auntie Sherry told the school that she'd bring me a change of clothes. She arrived shortly with my change of clothes and we headed toward the restroom so I could change. Once we were inside the restroom, Auntie Sherry pulled down my pants and gave me a good spanking because "big girls don't pee their pants." I'm sure that this wasn't the first nor would it be the last beating that I would have to endure.

At the age of four I also remember that Egg found a new boyfriend Eric. I hated him at first because the only man I wanted Egg to be with was Sperm. But as time passed I would grow to love him as if he was my father. The year of 1989 would also be the first time that I would witness Egg and her boyfriend doing drugs. I remember it like it was yesterday. I was dancing around in my living room to Snap "I got the power" video when I decided that I wanted a snack. I ran to Egg's bedroom and opened the door, and that's when I saw her and her boyfriend smoking something out of a pipe. I knew that they were doing something wrong because as soon as I entered the room they went into an instant panic and started looking for a place to hide the pipe. I would later learn that the something that they were smoking was Crack cocaine.

Egg and I lived in Forest Park for about a year, and then in 1990, we moved to Broadview, IL, and stayed in a one-bedroom apartment with Grandma Yolanda. I loved living in Broadview. It was like a family reunion all year round considering the fact that Grandma Mrs. Rolland (Grandma Yolanda's mother) and Uncle Ernest James (Grandma Yolanda's brother) lived upstairs and Auntie Ellen (Grandma Yolanda's sister) and her husband Otis lived right across the hall from us. I was now five years old and attending Roosevelt Elementary, which was only two blocks away from our apartment.

I remember one day after I came home from school I went into the bedroom as I always did, and began to jump up and down on the bed. I did this a couple of times and then I spotted a plate on top of the dresser. I stopped jumping and went over to the dresser and pulled the plate down. I didn't know what it was that was on the plate at the time, but I would soon learn that it was cocaine with a razor blade. Seeing that I didn't know what it was I took it to Egg, and continued jumping on the bed. Hours later, once Grandma Yolanda got home from work, they both took turns beating me. I couldn't understand why, all I had done was showed Egg the plate that I had found on top of the dresser.

Although we no longer lived in Forest Park, IL, Egg and her boyfriend Eric still kept in touch with each other and on August 8, 1991 they had a baby boy named Mitchell I was crushed; I was no longer the only child and, worst of all, no longer the center of attention. Sperm wasn't too fond of the idea that Egg had a baby with another man or the idea of another man being a father figure in my life. So, Sperm thought it would be a good idea to tell me that he was going to start picking me up on the weekends and spending time with me. I remember crying myself to sleep in a lawn chair on the back porch on one occasion as I waited for him to come and pick me up, but he never showed up. Uncle Donald surprised me the following week with a giant stuffed animal and five dollars.

Shortly after Mitchell was born, Auntie Sherry got hooked on drugs and the state of Illinois put her four children, Chantel, Eboney, Perry, and Chevonne, into foster care. They had no place to go, so Grandma

Yolanda took custody of them. The eight of us lived in a one-bedroom apartment. For years, I shared the top part of a bunk bed with Chevonne who was nine days younger than Mitchell, while Mitchell shared the bottom bunk with Perry who was six months younger than me, Chantel who was five years older than me and Eboney who was two years older than me shared a queen-sized bed, while Egg and Grandma Yolanda slept on the two couches in the living room.

Once again I was no long the center of attention. Egg sensed that I was overwhelmed with the changes that had happened and decided to throw me a surprise seventh birthday party at Chuck E. Cheese. It was spectacular; I remember all my cousins, first grade classmates, and even my first grade teacher Ms. Zaris showed up. But, the one person that I wanted to show up the most was Sperm, and he failed to attend. By this time, I had grown accustom to him no showing up, so I didn't shed a tear.

As time passed, I began to enjoy living in a household with five other children. I had been an only child for six years; I now had five other people to play with, and best of all, I now had five other people to point a finger at when something went wrong. As more time passed, Egg's drug habit got worse. I remember numerous times when she'd have me call Grandpa Barry and tell him that I needed money for school supplies and clothes. I'd never see the money nor would I ever receive the school supplies or clothes because Egg would receive the money. She'd just use it to support her drug habit. I believe the thing with Grandpa Barry was that he felt somewhat sympathetic to the fact that neither he nor Sperm were involved in my life, and figured that he could buy my love with money. Grandpa Barry soon caught on to Egg's tricks and then began to send his girlfriend Beth to take me school shopping.

At the age of seven, I was always a huge fan of school. I saw school as a way for me to get away from the painful life that I was living and a place that I could pretend to be someone else. If I had to choose my best year in elementary school, it would have to be second grade. I had Ms. Gore, the coolest second grade teacher ever, and I also met Dustin my first childhood crush. Dustin and I lived two blocks away from each other and, being that I was a major tomboy when I was younger, we'd play together all the time. Dustin and I soon decided that we were boyfriend and girlfriend. This didn't last long. Dustin soon broke up with me as well as started to make fun of me because his two older brothers told him that Egg was a "crackhead". I was crushed; Egg's drug use had caused me to lose my boyfriend, as well as my best friend. I remember crying about Dustin and telling Egg what happened and what he had said about her. Egg then told me to tell Dustin that "his dad smokes crack too, because I seen him buy it from the cab driver before".

During the summer of 1993, I remember that Egg told Mitchell and I that she couldn't stand living with seven other people in a one-bedroom apartment anymore. She told us that we were moving into our own place in Oak Park, IL. I was excited. Things were now going to be the way that I always wanted them to be: me, Mitchell, and Egg. We moved into a two-bedroom shelter in Oak Park, IL. It was an apartment with two bedrooms and one bathroom. My brother and I had to share a bedroom with Egg. A woman by the name of Brandy shared the other bedroom with her younger son Harley. This would only last a month, and then we'd move to Bellwood, IL.

I guess the shelter was only temporary, Egg had a one-month deadline to find a job and then an apartment for us to live in and of course she failed to meet it. After our month was up in Oak Park, we packed up and moved to Bellwood, IL, to live with Auntie Ellen and her husband Otis. Michael and I didn't even bother getting settled in because we knew that we wouldn't be there for long. Sure enough, we were only there for a couple of weeks and then we were booted out because Egg had begun to steal from Auntie Ellen and Uncle Otis to support her drug habit. Talk about biting the hand that feeds you. We moved back in with Grandma Yolanda in Broadview.

At the end of summer in 1994 I was eight years old and entering third grade. I would honestly have to say that I became somewhat of a problem child in third grade. Nothing major of course, I'd just come home late after school, talk back to my teacher, Ms. Keeves, get sent to the principal's office, and I was assigned a lot of detention. I remember one day Ms. Keeves pulled me out into the hallway and asked me why I was behaving so badly. I broke down and started to cry, I told her pretty much everything that I have written in this book so far.

This was extremely dumb for me to do, because as soon as I came home from school that day, Egg was waiting for me. As soon as I walked through the door I saw her standing there with a thick Black belt in her hand. There was no point in me asking what I had done because I already knew, and was now ready to suffer the consequences for telling the truth. Egg made me pull down my pants and lie face/chest down on one kitchen chair while my stomach/legs were laid across another kitchen chair and then began beating my bare ass with one of the thickest leather belts ever made. Egg and Grandma Yolanda had even named the belt "Slick Rick". The name was also engraved on the belt in big, bold silver metal letters. I assume that it must have belonged to someone by the name of Rick at one point of time. I honestly don't know whom the belt belonged to or where it came from. But I do know that it was the one thing that all of us kids feared the most. Needless to say, that after this beating, I learned at a very early age that I couldn't trust anyone, as well as to keep my mouth shut.

By this time Egg had taken to the liking of a new gentleman by the name of Alan. I honestly don't even remember Alan's last name not that it'd matter anyway considering the fact that within a year Mitchell and I would have a new brother who's father didn't even want him to have his last name. I didn't like Alan from the first day I met him, and this time it wasn't because I didn't want to see Egg with any other man besides Sperm. I was nine years old and could have cared less that Egg had found a new boyfriend. The reasoning behind me not liking Alan was more personal; I didn't like Alan because he reminded me of Sperm. It was everything, the way he looked, the way he walked, the tone of his voice, and most of all the way he smiled.

Once winter arrived, Egg decided that we'd move to the northside of Chicago to live with Auntie Lola who was actual Grandma Yolanda's aunt. We only lived with Auntie Lola for a couple of weeks. I don't exactly remember why we moved, but I'm pretty sure it had something to do with Egg's sticky fingers. We moved back to Broadview again and Egg met a new guy friend by the name of Nick.

Nick had moved into the same apartment building and lived upstairs from us with his grandmother. Nick was a GQ type of guy as well as a smooth talker, and Egg had become very fond of him. I remember that Nick would always come down to our apartment and party with both Egg and Grandma Yolanda. As time passed by Grandma Yolanda became very fond of Nick as well. Both Egg and Grandma Yolanda wanted what they couldn't have, which was Nick. Nick would use both Egg and Grandma Yolanda for drugs, alcohol, and even sex. It didn't take long before they both realized that they were being used and turned against each other.

At the age of nine, I'd witnessed many family fights before, Auntie Sherry and Uncle Ernest James, Uncle Ernest James and Auntie Ellen's son Wes, Auntie Sherry and Egg, Egg and Uncle Ernest James but this one was by far was the hardest to watch. I don't remember the exact date but I do know that it happened in January of 1995. Both Egg and Grandma Yolanda had been drinking and arguing all night long about Nick. My brother and I along with our four cousins sat and pretended that we couldn't hear them yelling at each other. We were all in the living room watching television, as they continued to yell at each other in the kitchen. We heard Egg yell, "I can't believe my own mother fucked my man." Then we heard Grandma Yolanda yell, "He ain't your man, Alan's supposed to be your man."

We then heard the sound of a struggle and before any of us could get up to see what was going on into the living room, they fell. Egg had Grandma Yolanda by her neck on the dining room table. From that point on it was complete mayhem. My brother and I along with my cousins, screamed in fear as they yelled at each other, punched each other, and pulled each other's hair. The front door to our apartment was open and as they struggled a little more, they made their way into the hallway, and that's when Egg kicked Grandma Yolanda down twelve stairs. The fall didn't even faze her because she got right back up and they were at it again. Finally, Chantel and Eboney pulled them away from each other and the fight was over. There was blood and hair everywhere. Grandma Yolanda yelled "pack up your shit and get the fuck out my house".

Once again we had to relocate, but it wasn't as bad as it had been before, because we moved right upstairs with Grandma Mrs. Rolland and Uncle Ernest James. Egg and Grandma Yolanda didn't speak to each other for about a month or so then they realized that it was dumb of them to fight over Nick. They finally patched things up and began to talk to each other again. They both knew that there was too much damage done and that things would never be the way that they used to be, but they still decided to give it a try any way. I believe that it was mostly for the sake of me, my brother, and our cousins.

March 4, 1995, was the day of my tenth birthday. I remember earlier that day Chantel was teasing me because she knew what Egg had gotten me for my birthday, but she wouldn't tell me. Hours later, and one dollar short from five, she finally told me what Egg had gotten me. Chantel told me that Egg had bought me a used bike for my birthday and that it was hidden in the basement and that she would take me to see it. I followed Chantel downstairs to the basement and watched as she open the door, and there it stood, it was a brown and silver ten-speed bike. I didn't have much growing up, so to me a used ten-speed bike was better than not having one at all. Chantel made me swear that I wouldn't tell Egg that she had told or showed me the bike, and I didn't

Later that night, once Egg got done eating, sleeping, and roaming streets, she finally came home and told me that she had a birthday gift for me. She then told me to come downstairs into the basement. By this time I could've cared less what she had for me: it was late, I was tired, and plus I already knew that she had bought me a used brown and silver ten-speed bike. But I went downstairs into the basement anyway and pretended to be surprised when she showed it to me. I never got a chance to ride the bike, and that night was the last time that I ever saw the bike because less than a week later Egg told me, "someone stole your bike out of the basement." I didn't buy that lie for a second, I knew that Egg sold my bike and bought crack with the money.

I was ten years old and Egg's drug habit was growing even worse as each day passed. It got to the point where I couldn't even bare to be around her anymore. I remember that I'd stay after school everyday and help my fourth grade teacher, Ms. Dicks clean, the entire classroom, and in return I'd get candy. I have to admit that the only reason why I helped Ms. Dicks clean was because I knew that she'd give me candy, and even more so because I knew that this way I wouldn't have to go straight home after school. This didn't last long because Egg didn't like the idea of me staying after school and ordered me to come directly home after school everyday.

Chapter 2

All Good Things Must Come to an End

In the summer of 1995 many things changed, but they all seemed like good changes at the time. Grandma Yolanda found a three-bedroom house in Maywood, IL. Grandma Yolanda even let me, my brother, and Egg move into her house. Once again, the eight of us were living together. This time it was under much better living conditions. My cousins and I were no longer crammed into one-bedroom because we now had three. Chantel, Eboney, and I shared the largest bedroom, and we each had our own bed. Perry and Mitchell shared another bedroom with bunk beds. Chevonne and Grandma Yolanda were practically joined together at the hip so; naturally they slept together in Grandma Yolanda's queen-sized bed. Egg slept on the couch in the living room.

That same summer I found out that Egg was pregnant by Alan. She was carrying a baby boy that was due in December. Egg didn't seem excited. Why would she be? Egg had already made it quite obvious that Mitchell and I were enough baggage for her to carry around. Egg being pregnant wasn't the only highlight for the summer, because this would be the summer that I would start to visit Northbrook, IL, where Mitchell's dad Eric and his girlfriend Rachel lived. For the past two years, Eric had been picking Mitchell up every weekend. I was always left behind until one weekend Eric invited me to come along. I gladly went with that day, and every weekend from that day on that Eric came to pick up Mitchell, I went with them as well.

At the age of ten Mitchell's dad Eric was the only father figure that I had ever had in my entire life and I will always have a great amount of respect for him because he always treated me as if I was his real daughter. Rachel was like the mother that Mitchell and I always dreamed of, and that's why I believe that Egg didn't like her. Rachel did everything perfect and Egg envied her for that so the only reason that she could come up with for not liking her was because she was White. The color of Rachel's skin didn't matter to my brother and I because we didn't care what she looked like on the outside; we loved her for who she was on the inside.

I can honestly say that the only time that I was truly happy was when my brother and I were with Eric and Rachel. We were the perfect family, and both my brother and I loved it, we'd always eat breakfast together, eat lunch together, eat dinner together, watch movies together, go for walks together, go shopping together, go swimming together, no matter what we did, we always did it together as a family. We'd go to Chuck E. Cheese, Midevil Times, and I even went to the movies for the first time in my life while in Northbrook. Eric and Rachel even bought me my first pair of rollerblades as well as taught me how to rollerblade. The weekends that my brother and I spent in Northbrook, IL with Eric and Rachel were like heaven here on earth.

On December 28, 1995, while Mitchell and I were visiting Northbrook, IL for Christmas we received a phone call from Egg telling us that she had just given birth to a baby boy by the name of Jayvon Nicholas. Although Jayvon's father was Alan, Nick was the one in the delivery room when he was born and that's why he was given Nicholas as his middle name and Egg's last name. Mitchell and I really didn't care that we had a new baby brother and I sure as hell didn't care either because I knew that that was just one extra child I'd have to baby-sit while Egg continued to rip and run the streets.

The year of 1996 was one of the worst years of my life. In January of 1996 one of Uncle Ernest James's friends who went by the name of Kurt began to visit our home in Maywood on a daily basis. I really didn't think much of it at first simply because he had been a friend of the family for years. My cousins and I were always excited when Kurt came around simply because he would always give us money as well as pictures of famous singers. Kurt was a professional photography, and any major concert that was held in Chicago, IL, Kurt was there snapping pictures. He would give us pictures of famous R&B such as: R. Kelly, LL Cool J, Changing Faces, Immature, Monica, and Brandy just to name a few. So in our eyes he was the coolest guy around.

Kurt was always a very touchy feely type of guy, everything from giving back massages, to tickling, and he always wanting my cousins and I to sit on his lap. But once again, I really didn't think anything of it. On this particular day in January Kurt came over to our house in Maywood to use his latest pictures. At a certain point, I remember that Kurt excused himself to go to the bathroom. Kurt had been gone for a while so I decided that I'd go and see what he was doing. As I walked to the back of house I noticed that the bathroom door was open and no one was in there. I then noticed that my bedroom light was mysteriously on so I walked into my room to shut it off, and that's where I found Kurt. He was standing there with a pair of panties in his hand, we caught eyes briefly and then I ran out of the room.

I went into the living room and sat next to my younger cousin Chevonne and continued to watch television. Kurt soon came into the living room and begun to watch television as well. As time passed by Kurt seemed to become anxious, and left the room again. I assumed that he went to the bathroom so Chevonne and I went to go and grab a couple of juice boxes out the refrigerator. As soon as we walked into the kitchen, there stood Kurt in the corner with his penis hanging out of the zipper part of his pants.

Chevonne and I were stunned, we didn't know what to do or say. We then left and went into my bedroom. I then looked at her and asked her what she had seen. It was true; she had seen the exact thing that I had seen. We then sat there a little bit longer debating on what actions needed to be taken. That's when we both decided that we had to go and tell Grandma Yolanda. We waited until she was by herself then we told her that we had witnessed Kurt exposing himself. She then asked us if we were sure and then told us that she would make him leave. Grandma Yolanda went into the living room and told Kurt that he had to leave because she was tired and ready to go to bed.

Whether Kurt realized it or not, the inappropriate gesture that Chevonne and I had witnessed him doing, had turned our family against each other. Grandma Yolanda and Egg believed us and no longer allow Kurt in the house. While Grandma Mrs. Rolland and Ernest James believed Kurt and still allowed him to come over. I remember I was visiting Grandma Mrs. Rolland once and Kurt came over, I was in shock, I didn't know what to do or say. So, I pretended as if he wasn't even there. But of course there came a point in time where it was just Kurt and I, that's when he turned to me and said "Timesha, I don't know what you think you saw, but what ever you think you saw, you should have pretended like you didn't see it." Once again I learned that I couldn't trust anyone as well as to keep my mouth shut.

By the time spring came around I was now eleven years old and the mother of two. I say that I was the mother of two simply because Egg had gotten into heavy drug and alcohol use and I was the only mother that my brothers knew. I remember one evening I was asked to baby-sit my two brothers Mitchell and Jayvon along with Egg's best friend Mia two sons. Originally, Mia's older son Marcus was suppose to baby-sit but decided that he wanted to stay the night at one of his friend's house. I was then forced to baby-sit while Egg, Mia, and her boyfriend Ted went out to the clubs. After hours of feeding, changing diapers, and chasing around four boys between the ages of three months and six years old, I was now able to get some rest considering the fact that I had school in the morning. I laid down on the living room floor and watched music videos until I eventually feel asleep.

I don't know exactly when or why Marcus came home that night, but I do know that it was almost morning when he woke me up because I remember the sun was slightly shining through the window. I awoke to the sound of 112 featuring The Notorious B.I.G "only you" video and Marcus on top of me. He was on top of me pulling and tugging at my clothing, and I knew what was happening. I was raped at the age of eleven by Egg's best friend's fifteen-year-old son. This would be the first of many times that I'd get raped by Marcus. I never told anyone, because at the time he was dating my older cousin Chantel but most of all because, if no one believed that Kurt had exposed himself to me then they sure as hell wouldn't believe that Marcus had raped me. I later learned that I wasn't Marcus's only victim when a friend of Mia's daughter named Rihanna became pregnant by Marcus. I never talked to Rihanna about it, but to this day I still believe that her pregnancy was the result of her being raped like I had been.

Spring was now over with and summer had just begun. Mitchell and I had gotten tired of our living condition and decided that we were going to go and live with Mitchell's dad and his girlfriend in Northbrook, IL. I was eleven and Mitchell was five, neither one of us were able to drive so we decided that we'd walk to Northbrook, IL, which was about an hour drive. Needless to say, we knew that we had a long walk ahead of us but we didn't care, we just wanted to start a new life. It was a sunny Saturday afternoon when Mitchell and I left Brodview, we stopped by a local gas station to pick up some snacks for our journey, and off we went. We must have been walking on the highway for at least two hours.

We climbed many fences in order to keep away from all of the traffic and many cars drove by and asked us if we needed a ride but we declined each time because we didn't want to take a ride from strangers. We walked and ran, ran and walked, until we became very tired, but we refused to give up, we had to make it to Northbrook before dark. We were finally rescued when a Westchester police officer was called to investigate "two kids walking on the highway". Mitchell and I had made it all the way to Westchester, IL. Now I don't know how far Westchester is from Brodview, but it sure as hell isn't right around the corner.

I don't remember the name of the officer that picked us up, but he was very kind and understanding. He asked if Mitchell and I were hungry and we told him that we were and he bought us each a Happy meal from McDonalds. Afterwards, we told him why we were running away from home and that we needed to get to Northbrook, IL. Mitchell and I both cried and begged him to give us a ride to Northbrook, but he told us that he wasn't allowed to and that someone would have to come and pick us up. I tried calling Mitchell's dad but I couldn't remember the phone number. We had no other choice but to call Egg. When Egg arrived she paraded around the room as if she was the perfect mother in the world, apologized to the officer for what we had done. Mitchell and I watched in disgust, aware that the way she was acting was far from the way she would be acting once she got us home. As soon as we arrived home the beatings began for both of us. Egg told us that we were being punished for our own good.

Also in the summer of 1996, I was now entering the sixth grade, so I thought. To my surprise once I arrived at Roosevelt Elementary, I was informed that Egg had called the school and said that she felt that "Timesha didn't learn enough in fifth grade" and advised the school to make me repeat the fifth grade. There are no words in the world to describe how I felt that day. I was so humiliated with the fact that all of the kids that I had known since kindergarten were going into sixth grade and I was left behind repeating fifth. But most of all I was pissed at Egg. How dare her order the school to make me repeat fifth grade. If Egg had truly felt that I didn't learn enough in fifth grade maybe she should have took a break from drinking her 40oz and put down her crack pipe and taught me what she felt I needed to learn. This is something that I will never forget and always hate her for. Egg didn't even graduate high school, but she felt the need to make me repeat fifth grade. I don't understand how Egg would dare try to give advice about my life when she isn't even practicing what she's preaching.

It seems like whenever you think that things couldn't get any worst, they always do. In the fall of 1996, after a night of drinking, Grandma Yolanda went to bed and woke up the next morning only to realize that she couldn't move the right side of her body. She had suffered from a stroke while she was sleeping and the entire right side of her body was paralyzed. Grandma Yolanda had always been the one and only person that kept the family together and now it was every man for himself.

Grandma Yolanda had always been very independent and now she was as helpless as a newborn baby. We had to help her do everything including feeding her, bathing her, dressing her, helping her to the restroom, helping her walk, helping her learn how to write with her left hand, and she even had to take speech classes because her speech was so impaired. But, I didn't mind because after all, Grandma Yolanda was always the one person who took us in when everyone else kicked us out. I felt that it was the least I could do.

In January of 1997 Egg and Grandma Yolanda had an argument that would alter the lives of the entire household. Once again we were we kicked out due to Eggs sticky fingers along with many other reasons. Egg decided that we'd go back to where it all began, Chicago, IL. Egg along with my brothers and I moved back to the west side of Chicago in the exact house that I lived in for the first three years of my life. I must admit that I was excited that I would be living in the same house as Sperm. But that happiness would soon disappear due to the fact that he was just as deep if not deeper into drugs as Egg.

My brothers and I rarely came out of the room that we slept in. The only time that we'd come of our room was to eat, use the restroom, watch television when no one else was home, and go to school. Mitchell and I attended school a couple of blocks up the street. We hated having to attend a new school, the students weren't very friendly to new comers and we were both made fun everyday. We always had to walk to school together because we lived on the worst side of Chicago. Not to mention we were living in a crack house, with crack users, and had to endure the sound of gunshots as we tried to sleep the night away. My brothers and I went to bed each night not knowing if we'd even live to see another day. We wouldn't have to live like this for much longer.

In the winter of 1996 right before we moved to Chicago, IL Egg had meet a new guy friend by the name of Tory. They met when Tory came down to Broadview, IL from Minnesota due to his mother passing away. Egg kept in contact with Tory while we were living in Chicago, and one day she told my brothers and I to pack up all of our stuff because we were moving to Minnesota. Egg hardly knew this man and she had us packing our bags so we could go relocate to another state and live with her so called boyfriend.

We made a trip back to Broadview as well as Maywood Illinois before we left for Minnesota. That's when Grandma Yolanda told me that I didn't have to go and that I could stay with her. As much as I would have loved to stay and live with her I just couldn't do it. I was the only mother that my brothers had ever known, and I knew that if I was to stay in

Illinois and send them off to Minnesota with Egg, that they would've been as good as dead. I had no choice but to go, my brothers needed me there to protect them, because in their eyes I was their mother.

Grandpa Barry dropped us off at the bus station, paid for our tickets, bought us food for the bus ride, gave Egg some extra cash, and then it was time for us to leave. I remember that I was crying and that my grandfather had tears in his eyes as he wiped mine away and told me not to cry. I watched my grandfather walk away as the bus drove off. As of today that was the last time I ever saw my grandfather. We left the bus station at noon and took the Greyhound bus from Chicago, IL, then switched over to a Jefferson bus in Tomah, WI, and finally made it to Minnesota nine hours later. I don't remember much of the bus ride because I had cried so much that I cried myself to sleep.

I don't remember the exact day that we arrived in Minnesota but I do know that it was the first week in February. It was around nine at night, and there we stood outside of a Conoco gas station in Minnesota. After, about twenty minutes or so, Tory arrived to pick us up in a yellow taxicab. We gathered all of our belonging and threw them into the trunk of the cab, took a sit and enjoyed the ride. We were all very tired from the nine hour long bus ride, and decided to call it a night. The next day would be a day that neither Mitchell nor I would ever forget.

Chapter 3
Welcome to Minnesota

Our first day in Minnesota, was the day that Egg almost killed Mitchell. Mitchell was five years old at the time and like most five-year-old boys, he was very curious. Mitchell had gone to use the bathroom, and while he was in there he decided to squirt liquid hand soap all over a Glade plug in, and then stick it in the bathroom electrical socket. You can pretty much guess what happen next, all the lights went out in the entire house and Egg went into an immediate rage. Egg opened the bathroom door and asked Mitchell what he had done, and he told her. Jayvon and I then watched as she pulled Mitchell out of the bathroom by the back of his neck, through him onto the bedroom floor, picked him up again by the back of his neck and then threw him onto the bed and started beating him non-stop.

I watched. Jayvon watched. We both watched in fear not knowing what to do as Mitchell screamed at the top of his lungs. All of a sudden Egg stopped beating Mitchell and started to choke him. I couldn't watch any longer, I had to intervene. So, I ran and jumped on top of Egg's back and began trying to pull her off of him. I vowed that second to myself that I would never speak of this day again. It was extremely hard for me to watch so I can't even imagine what it must have been like for Mitchell to go through it. Neither Mitchell nor I would ever speak of this day until five years later.

As soon as we had moved to Minnesota, within two weeks, we were leaving. We didn't care that we were moving nor were we surprised that we were moving, simply because moving around was all that we had ever known. I guess that things weren't working out between Egg and Tory. Maybe it was because Tory was out working all day while Egg just lay around his house all day and did nothing, or maybe it was because Egg had started hanging out at a local battered women's center and had found out that Tory had a thing for beating up women. Whatever the case was, we were now moving to La Crosse, WI to live in a shelter for battered women. I really couldn't understand why we were living in a battered women's shelter when Egg had never been battered. It wouldn't matter anyway seeing that we would only live there for a month, and this shelter is where I would celebrate my twelfth birthday.

It was now towards the middle of March of 1997 and we were back living in Minnesota at a shelter for women and their children. As usual we were only allowed to stay at the shelter for one month and once our month was up we would be living out of a motel. We lived at the motel for a little over two weeks and then May 1st came.

May 1, 1997 was the day that we moved a low-income apartment complex. The complex was designed for people with low income and consisted of about twenty townhouses that contained four separate apartments with each one ranging from two to four bedrooms. We lived in a three-bedroom, one bathroom townhouse, and for once my brothers and I were happy because for the very first time in our lives we now had a place of our own that we could truly call home. Our happiness wouldn't last long. For a split second I thought that Egg had cleaned up her act and kicked her bad habits to the curb. Silly me, Egg hadn't stopped drinking or smoking crack; she was just low on cash for a while and didn't know of anywhere or anyone that she could buy drugs from. That is until she met Richard.

Richard was Egg's soon to be boyfriend who by the way was White. I found this to be extremely interesting considering just a few years back, Egg was the one and only person who seemed to have a problem with Mitchell's dad having a White girlfriend, but now a few years later it's ok for her too have a White boyfriend, sounds to me like the pot's trying to call the kettle Black. I don't exactly remember how they met, but my brothers and I liked him a lot. We didn't have any problems with him other than the fact that Egg was never home with us anymore because she was always with him. Richard lived right up the street from our apartment in a local trailer court. This is where Egg spent most of her time drinking and doing drugs. Egg was never able to hold down a job longer that a month because she was always to busy getting drunk and high all the time, plus she wouldn't have money for transportation to work because what little money she had went towards beer and crack.

The summer of 1997 is when I saw first hand how selfish, self centered, and inconsiderate of others that Egg truly was. In the summer of 1997 there was a really bad storm; one might even say that it was a small tornado. Roofs were blown off, the power went out, countless trees were all over the roads, and the town was flooded like you wouldn't believe. Anyone could have easily guessed where Egg was while all of this was going on, Richard's trailer. Egg could have cared less that my brothers and I were huddled together, crying in a dark basement scared out of our minds not knowing if we were going to live or die. We had never been through anything like this in our entire lives and the one person that we needed the most, Egg wasn't even there to comfort us.

The summer of 1997 passed by quickly as did fall and winter. It was now mid February of 1998 and Egg decided that Mitchell was causing too much trouble and that he needed to get some professional help. Mitchell was sent to a hospital in Rochester or Red Wing, MN to undergo many tests to try and come to an explanation as to why he was behaving so badly. Mitchell would spend a month in the hospital only to be diagnosed with ADHD. I've never said anything to anyone but believe that a majority of Mitchell's behavior problems were drug related.

I remember that at the age of four, I caught Egg and Mitchell's dad smoking crack, and I know for a fact that she continued to smoke crack while she was pregnant with Jayvon. Mitchell and I fought a lot growing up but when he was gone for a month I truly realized how much I loved him. I remember that Egg and I went to visit him at the hospital that the second I saw so him and he gave me a hug and my eyes filled with tears.

I know it may sound weird but I felt like I was a mother whose son had been taking away from her.

I had too much pride to let a tear drop out of my eye, plus I've always been the type of person to say, "crying just shows a sign of weakness". So, I just kept my feelings as well as everything else bottled up inside. I found it extremely hard to do simple things that I had done everyday. I found it even harder to celebrate my thirteenth birthday without my big brother Mitchell. I had grown accustom to always having him there to living the party up by dancing all over the place. Things just weren't the same with him being gone.

The summer of 1998 would be the first time that I'd get arrested by the police as well as put on probation. It was a warm and sunny in June and my brothers were outside in our front yard playing with their friends. I was inside watching television when all of a sudden the front door to our house swings open and through the door runs Mitchell crying. I asked Mitchell what had happen and that when he replied "the lady next door just called me a little Nigger". Everything else from that point on was a blur. All I remember is that I walked out of my house went and knocked on my neighbor's door, and when she opened it I lost all self-control. The only thing I remember is pulling her by her hair outside the door, down four stairs onto the ground and the fight was on!

At the age of thirteen I would have done anything for my brothers even if it meant sacrificing my own life. And after what Egg had done to Mitchell back in February of 1997, I vowed that no one would ever hurt my little brother again. So when Mitchell told me what had happened I had no choice but to attack. After the fight was over with, Egg somehow found out what had happened and for the first time in her life decides that she needs too protect Mitchell as well. By this time the police were called to the scene, Egg and I were both fighting with the police and in return we were both arrested and taken to jail. I was a minor at the time so I only had to stay at the police station for a couple of hours, while Egg had to stay there for the entire weekend.

July of 1998 was when I was introduced to a twenty-three year old woman by the name of Kelly. Kelly was a college student who attended college at the local university, but also worked as a mentor for the county.

When I was put on probation I agreed to do community service, take anger management classes, and get a mentor/big sister. I loved having Kelly as a mentor simply because I was able to get away from the shit hole that I called home. The one day a week that I spent with Kelly was like a dream come true, we'd do many exciting things such as: going to the movies, going out to eat, visiting the library, or even something as simple as going for a walk. Kelly was my new best friend as well as my mentor, who would later become my mom.

Summer was now over and fall was here, and things were about to change. It was now the beginning of October and my brothers and I were going into foster care for a month while Egg would be in Red Wing, MN receiving treatment for her alcohol abuse. She had the choice of going to rehab or losing custody of all three of us. Mitchell had done his time back in the spring of 1998 and now it was her turn. During the month that Michael had spent in Rochester or Red Wing, MN he didn't think twice about telling his doctors whatever they wanted to know. I didn't mind that we were going into foster care simply because I had been taken care of my brothers for so many years and I needed a break.

October 1, 1998 is when my brothers and I met Suzanne and Robert Hall. The Hall's would be our mom and dad for a month while Egg was in rehab. I took a liking to Robert right away simply because he has a great sense of humor. I loved joking around, so a great sense of humor was something that we had in common. Now, Suzanne was a different story, the moment I met her I felt a strange vibe. The way she acted, and the things she said just led me to believe that she wasn't too fond of me. But within months, would find out that my instincts were right.

I've always been the type of person who actually enjoys being alone. Suzanne, found this to be disturbing and then called my mentor Kelly and asked her to come over to talk to me. I explained to Kelly that I kept to myself because I got a strange vibe from Suzanne and that I didn't feel comfortable around her. Suzanne also didn't like the idea that Jayvon, who was three at the time, was so dependent on me. I became aware of this first day that we moved into their home. The original plan was for Jayvon to sleep in the same room as me, because that's what he wanted and I was fine with that idea. That's when Suzanne decided that Jayvon was too old to be sleeping in the same bed as his sister. In the end Suzanne won and we both had separate rooms as well as beds.

During the month that we lived with the Hall's, my brothers and I went to visit Egg in rehab. I really didn't want to go but I had to. As soon as my brothers and I arrived, Egg met us outside and the show began. Egg had never met the Hall's before so she introduced herself and thanked them for taking care of us. But as soon as we went inside the hospital and up to her room the shit talking began. She went on and on about how the state of Minnesota thinks that their going to take us away from her, how Robert was too good looking to be married to Suzanne, how Mitchell's social worker Margi was the bitch that put her in rehab, and how she couldn't wait to get out and start drinking again. Our visit with Egg was pointless considering the fact that the only thing we did was listen to her bitch non-stop for two hours. Needless to say, all three of us were extremely excited to leave when the Hall's came back to pick us up.

Overall, I would honestly have to say that the month I spent living in the Hall's home was the most peaceful as well as stress free month in my life. It was like heaven, I didn't have to cook, clean, change dirty diapers, and best of all I didn't have to be a mom. I now had people to take care of me as well as my brothers; this was something that was foreign to all three of us. The month I spent living in the Hall household was a great experience and I wouldn't trade it for anything else in the world.

Chapter 4

Some People Never Change

Once Egg was released from rehab, she stayed true to herself and started drinking as soon as she was back home. Thousands of dollars gone down the drain, money that could have been used to help someone who actually wanted to receive help. I think the one thing that people fail to realize is that you can't force someone to get help, that's something that the individual who needs help must do on their own.

I noticed, as I became a teenager that Egg started to envy me. I still don't understand how someone could be jealous of his or her own child. Aren't you supposed to wish for the best for your child? Aren't you supposed to want your child to have everything that you didn't have growing up, plus more? This wasn't the case with Egg. It was like she went to rehab and came back ten times worst.

She now had a great amount of hatred build up inside of her. She always had hate for Mitchell and I, but now she had just as much hate for Baby J. Baby J is the nickname that she made up for Jayvon because he was her "one and only baby boy". I remember waking up late one night to the sound of my brothers crying because Egg was in a drunken rage threaten to kill all of us including herself. She said that she would "wait until late at night when all three of you are sleeping, pour lighter fluid all over the house, and the light a match". My brothers were terrified, but I wasn't I knew that she was just bluffing, and that she was too much of a coward to ever do anything of that nature.

I also remember one night in mid November; I was still hungry after Egg had made dinner. This was far from a surprise considering the fact that everyone who knows me will agree that I'm a human vacuum cleaner. Plus, my brothers and I weren't used to Egg being home to cook so we thought of it as a special occasion. It was far from a special occasion, when I asked Egg for a second helping of food she called me a "gritty, ungrateful bitch" then told me that "if you don't like how I'm running things then you can get the fuck out my house".

Who would've known that asking for a second helping of food would turn into such a disaster? It was quite obvious that this situation was about to get ugly as well as the fact that I wasn't about to get a second helping of food. So I told her never mind and decided to excuse myself from the table because I really wasn't in the mood to argue. Big mistake, Egg saw this as me being disrespectful and kicked me out of the house. Literally! She grabbed me by the back of my neck, pushed me out the front door, and then kicked me in my back down the stairs.

I remember that the snow had fallen early that year. It was cold; I didn't have a coat, and had no clue what to do. So, I decided to walk up the street to a local grocery, and use the pay phone to call the one person that I knew would help me, Kelly, my mentor. She came and picked me up right away, we went to her house and she then called the police. Two police officers arrived shortly, we talked about what had happened, but in the end the final decision was for me to return home. I didn't want to go back, and Kelly didn't want me to go back home either, she told the officer that I could stay the night at her house instead.

I arrived home with a police escort, went straight upstairs to my room and waited for Egg to get done bullshitting the police officer and come upstairs and beat me. As soon as Egg walked into my room I knew what time it was, I took my beating like a soldier, and then proceeded to fall asleep. It was hard for me to fall asleep as I had to endure at least an hour of Egg yelling at me from downstairs, "and if you ever call the cops again and risk getting my boys taking away from me, I swear to God that I'll fucking kill you".

It was now towards the end November and this is around the time that Egg introduced my brothers and I to three young drug dealers from Chicago, IL. I assume that Egg had been buying crack from: P.J who was twenty-three years old, his older brother Ronny who was twenty-seven, and their younger cousin Jason who was nineteen for quite sometime. So after awhile Egg decided that it was dumb for them to pay for motel rooms every night and that they could live with us instead. Egg didn't mind that they were selling drugs out of our home, and why would she seeing that they were giving her free crack rocks here and there.

Mitchell and I both knew what was going on but there was nothing that we could do about it. My brothers and I had no problem with P.J, Ronny, and Jason living with us. Neither did my two girlfriends Fallon and Tamara who were both seventeen years old. Fallon had taken a liking to Ronny and had begun to sell drugs out of her home for him, while Tamara and Jason seemed to hit things off as well and she began to sell drugs out of her home for him as well. So, the only person that was left out in the cold was P.J. But that wouldn't be for long.

I know it might sound weird, but to me it seems like the more you hang around a person and get to know them, the more you start to like them or maybe even become attracted to them. This is what I believed to be true in the case with P.J and I. I wouldn't say that we were in love with each other because I know that wasn't the case at all. But there was some kind of unexplainable connection there, regardless of our ten-year age difference. And in January of 1999, I voluntarily had sex with a man who was ten years my senior. This would be one of three times that we would have sexual intercourse.

It was like our little secret, I didn't even have to tell Fallon or Tamara because they just knew, and I know that P.J wouldn't dare tell anyone considering the fact that he was now engaging in two illegal activities: selling drugs and having sex with a underage girl. I soon began to notice that both Fallon and Tamara always had new clothes as well as a lot of money to spend. I then knew what needed to be done, so in February of 1999, I agreed to start selling drugs for my twenty-three year old male friend.

I was a thirteen-year-old drug dealer. P.J would sell drugs when he was in Minnesota, and whenever he would go back to Illinois for a week or so to get more drugs, I would then be in charge of selling drugs for him in Minnesota until he got back. I must have sold drugs for almost three month, and I must admit that the pay off was great, I always had money in pocket, I got new clothes and shoes, I got my first CD player, I ate out all the time, and for each trip that P.J took back to Chicago, he brought me back a few crisp one hundred dollar bills.

My selling drugs also allowed me to truly see how bad Egg was strung out on crack. Egg knew that I was selling drugs and said that it was fine, but whenever P.J would go out of town she would always hound me for drugs. I must admit that Egg had never been nicer to me than she did during the three months that I was selling crack cocaine. I knew that it was all an act, I just had something that she wanted but didn't have enough money to buy. She'd always give me the sorrow trip by saying "you should give me drugs for free because I'm your mom" or "just spot me a bag now and I'll pay you back later" and of course my favorite line "just tell P.J that you lost one, he'll believe you".

I'd give Egg and free crack rock here and there mostly so she'd shut up, leave me alone, and get the hell out of my face. She would beg me non-stop and when I didn't give in she'd become very angry and say "I can't believe that you're choosing a man over you own mother". This lead me to believe that she knew all along that P.J and I were having sex together, but chose to say nothing. The thing she failed to realize is that I was nothing like her; she had always chosen men over my brothers and I. But, this was a different situation I had a job to do, and had to sell and certain amount of drugs and come up with a certain amount of money, it was as simple as that. To this day I still don't understand how a drug that's half the size of my pinky nail can take complete control of someone life.

The month of March started out good, I remember that my fourteenth birthday was on a Friday, P.J had given me money to buy myself a new outfit, and by chance that Friday March 4th was the day that the entire eight grade class went on a all day field trip to a Roller skating ring But the good times wouldn't last for long. On March 21st, I hit Egg for the first time in my life. Even though Egg caused my brothers and I a great deal of pain, and with all the cruel things that she did to me, this is something that I would have never thought would happen. Me hitting her back.

It happened one night when Egg was drunk as usual, and we got into an argument. She proceeded to call me numerous names such as "bitch", "slut", "whore", and of course I can't forget her favorite line that she got off of The Bill Cosby Show "I brought you in this world and I'll take you out". I sat on the couch and watched television with my brothers as she continued to yell. This made her even more pissed because she felt that I was ignoring her. Out of no where she jumps over the couch on top of me and begins punching me. What was I to do? Here she was drunk and ready to fight. I had no choice, hitting her back was the only way to get her off of me.

My brothers screamed in fear as we fought, just by chance my friend Fallon was visiting and broke the fight up. Egg didn't even have to say "get the fuck out my house", this time because I voluntarily left. I went to my friend Diana's house that lived up the street. Like clockwork, Egg soon came beating on her door looking for me. Diana told her that I wasn't there and that she hadn't seen me all night, I just knew that Egg was about to search her house for me, but she didn't. Instead she left a message for Diana to give to me the next time she saw me, "well whenever you see or hear from the bitch, tell her she's fucking dead. Can you believe that this bitch had the nerve to hit me back"?

The next morning the police came over to Diana's house looking for me, so I had no choice but to return back home. As soon as I was back home and the police left, Egg walked up to me and punched me in my face and said "you didn't think that I was actually going to let you get away with punching me in my jaw did you"? The punch didn't hurt at all, but I still pretended to cry just so she would leave me alone.

Later on that night Mitchell told me that "mom went crazy when you left last night, all she kept saying was that she couldn't believe that you hit her back. But I don't blame you I would've done the same thing too". Mitchell also informed me that Egg had trashed the house, broke an 8X10 picture frame with my picture of me in it, and even made both Mitchell and Jayvon pack their bags because they were "moving back to Illinois and leaving me behind in Minnesota".

I also found out from Richard that on that same night Egg had gone over to his trailer looking for me. He told me that she came over all drunk beating on his door. Richard said that he had been sleeping so it took him awhile to get up and answer the door. That's when Egg took it upon herself to throw a brick through his window, and then kick down his door yelling "you better let me the fuck in, because I already know Timesha's in there, and I know you're fucking her". Unbelievable, Egg swore to God that I was in a trailer having sex with her boyfriend. Talk about someone having low self-esteem.

One afternoon in April, Mitchell and I came home from school then went to pick Jayvon up from the daycare that he attended, as we had always done. When we arrived back home Egg wasn't there, no big deal she was never home anyway. Once we were inside of the house we noticed that none of the light switches worked. It then became very clear to me that Egg hadn't paid the electricity bill. As hours passed by we all began to wonder where Egg was. But Egg never came home that night; instead she came home around eight o'clock the following morning because she had spent her entire day and night with Richard.

Egg had no idea what my brother and I had gone through the night before. I had to gather up what little money I had at the time, and my brothers and I walked a couple blocks up the street to the grocery store and bought some food from the hot deli because we were hungry, and had no electricity to cook anything. We pretty much ate in the dark as we sat on our living room floor in front of a table with one candle burning as our only source of light. I'll never forget that the three of us slept on one couch in our living room with the front door open hoping that Egg would come home. But she never did, and this is something that I will never forgive her for as well as something that I will never forget.

Chapter 5
May 1, 1999

The afternoon of May 1, 1999, is the day that would forever change the lives of both my brothers and I. May 1, 1999 would be the day that our cry for help would finally be heard. May 1, 1999 was the day that everything would finally come to an end. May 1, 1999 was the day that the Police Department raided our house as well as Fallon's. The police had been watching our house for quite sometime, and had even sent police informants to our home to buy drugs. I guess the informant had bought drugs from my house enough times, and now the police department had enough evidence to raid our house.

The afternoon of May 1, 1999 was on a Saturday, and started out as a beautiful day. I remember that I had gotten up early that morning because I was planning on attending a barbecue with couple of my friends. Mitchell had gotten up early as well and was already out and about at one of his buddy's house that lived down the street. Jayvon and I watched cartoons, and then ate a bowl of cereal together. P.J and Jason had gone back to Chicago to get more drugs, so the only other people in the house were Egg and Ronny. Egg and Ronny were both downstairs in the basement, and everyone who ever came into our home knew that the basement was the place were all the illegal drug activities occurred.

After breakfast, Jayvon went back to watching his cartoons, while I headed outside to check on some clothes that were hanging on a clothesline. As soon as I walked outside of my back door I heard a strange sound, it's hard to describe the sound, but it was sort of like the sound of a stampede. Just as I peaked around the corner, I heard "Put your hands in the air and get on the Fucking ground now"! As I stood there with four big men in front of me, all dressed in Army clothing, with big boots, and head gear on and four gun barrows pointed at my face, I had no problem doing as I was told me. I then realized that my house was being raided and that the sound that I had heard just seconds before was the sound of the Swat team running down the street to raid my house like soldiers running onto the battle field to fight in a war.

I watched many officers as well as K9 dogs pour from around the corner, one stood in front of me with a Battering Ram in his arms. I suppose the officers thought that they would have to knock down our doors, but there would be no need for Battering Rams because at the time of the raid both of our doors were open as well as unlocked. Once both Egg and Ronny were apprehended from inside the house I was then allowed get off the ground. There was no need for me to even ask what was going on because I was fully aware that my house was being raided.

Once I was allowed to get off the ground the only thing that I was concerned about was my younger brother Jayvon. I already knew that Egg and Ronny were inside the house with police officers and that Mitchell was down the street at one of his friend's house, and although I continued to ask, no one seemed to know where Jayvon was. After about five minutes or so, I decided to walk up the stairs and look into my house, and to my surprise, sitting at the kitchen table was a scared and very confused two and a half year old. By this time there were at least twelve officers in the kitchen and living room alone, I asked one of the men standing in the kitchen if he would let Jayvon come outside with me and he said that was fine.

Now that I knew Jayvon was safe, my new main focus was Mitchell. Was Mitchell still at his friend's house? Did he have any idea what was going on? All these questions were running through my head. But I wouldn't be able to go and search for him simply because I wasn't allowed to leave the spot in which I was found. I stood at the top step of the back door of our house and watched as the police officers demolished what little belongings we had, when all of a sudden the front door to the house swung open, and through the door runs Mitchell with three officers chasing after him. To this day I still don't know exactly why Mitchell stormed through the door the way he did, but I do know that May 1, 1999 could have easily been the day that he lost his life.

Once Mitchell was apprehended by the officers, he then came and joined Jayvon and I outside of the house. By this time I was sitting on a picnic table watching Jayvon play on the slide at the park that was located directly behind our house. Mitchell came out and sat next to me and we sat in silence. After about almost three hours, Egg came out of the house and told us that she was going to jail and that we would be staying with Mallory and Leslie.

Mallory and Leslie were two women that my brothers and I knew very well. We met both Mallory and Leslie back in 1997 when we first moved to Minnesota, and had kept in touch with them. Mallory had three kids of her own: Chris who was a year older than me, Brady who was the same age as Mitchell, and Meagan who was a year older than Jayvon. Leslie had no kids and she and Mallory had been living with each other for years. They would make frequent trips to our house to visit and they would always come to my house and pick me up whenever I needed to do school work at their house on their computer. They even took me on a weekend trip with their family to St. Paul, MN to visit the Mall of America. This was extremely exciting seeing that I had never been to the Mall of America and we got to stay in a nice hotel with a swimming pool, hot tub, and recreation room. So, once Egg said that my brothers and I would be staying with them for a while, we were all excited.

Mallory and Leslie arrived within twenty minutes and my brothers and I hopped into their car, as the car pulled away we watched as two officers escorted Ronny out of the house and as another put Egg into handcuffs. The following day, which was a Sunday, Mallory and Leslie brought my brothers and I back to our house so that we could get enough clothes to last us for a week. But my brothers and I wouldn't need clothes for a week nor would we even be living with Mallory and Leslie for a week. We only lived with them for three days. I don't know exactly why we only lived with them for three days, but I do know that the three days that we spent

42

with them were three of my happiest days, as well as the last three days that I would ever live in the same household as my brother.

On Tuesday, May 4, 1999 at 3:00pm the school bell rang and school was now out for the day. As I walked out the door of Mrs. Smith's eighth grade math class, Kelly, my mentor, greeted me. At this time Kelly told me that my brothers and I would no longer be living with Mallory and Leslie. She also told me that my brothers would be going to live with Suzanne and Robert Hall and that I couldn't go and live with them because the Hall's were only licensed to have three kids at a time and that they had already had a teenage girl by the name of Maria living with them. In due time I would find out that this was all a lie. Kelly then told me that she would be more than willing to go to the County Courthouse and get a license to be my foster mom and that I could then come and live with her and her boyfriend if I wanted too.

Kelly telling me that I could come and live with her was like a dream come true. I then said, "Yes, I'd love to come and live with you"! It really met a lot to me that she was inviting a kid that she really knew nothing about into her home. Kelly and I had known each other for ten months, and the only things that she really knew about me were all bad things that somehow involved the County. This didn't seem to bother Kelly at all because she told me that "deep down inside I know that you're a good kid". And this is one of the reasons why I admire her the most, because she was willing to take a chance with a kid that she knew nothing about.

I then asked Kelly how she had found out what happen and she told me that she had a feeling that something was wrong because when she went to pick me up for our visit on Monday I wasn't there. She then told me that on the following day that Mitchell's social worker Margi called her in the early afternoon and asked her if she'd be willing to let me come and live with her and that the Hall's would let Mitchell and Jayvon come live with them. Kelly told me that she didn't think twice before telling Margi "yes".

My brothers and I had no immediate family in Minnesota, so the county had no choice but to put us in foster care. All of our family members including our fathers, grandparents, great grandparents, as well as aunts and uncles, lived in Illinois. None of this would matter in the end anyway because the following week when Margi got in contact with all three of our fathers as well as our grandparents, no one wanted us. It wasn't that Grandma Yolanda didn't want us it was just that she couldn't have us. Due to the stroke that she had back in 1996 that left the entire right hand side of her body paralyzed, she wasn't even able to take care of herself. Because of this, in 1997 the state of Illinois took Chantel, Eboney, Perry, and Chevonne away from her and put them into foster care.

In May of 1999, Grandma Yolanda was still trying to recover from her stroke, Grandma Mrs. Rolland was living in a nursing home and could barely remember the names of her own children, Grandpa Barry business was running fine I'd assume since he was able to afford a Cadillac as well as a Lexus, all of our aunts and uncles were strung out on drugs, and both Sperm and Jayvon's dad Alan were hooked on drugs as well. But the one thought that kept going through my head was "What about Mitchell's dad? He had always been so good to all three of us for so many years, why wouldn't he at least come and rescue his son? That's something that I didn't understand then and something that I will probably never understand. I guess something's are better left unexplained.

I must admit that it felt like someone stabbed me in the stomach once I found out that my brothers and I were being separated. Up until this point in time we had been together our entire lives, and now we were being torn apart. But that's when I looked at the bright side, even though all three of us couldn't be together, at least my brothers could be together, and as for me, I'd be fine on my own, because after all it was what I had grown accustom to and I'd been doing it for years. But, I also looked at the good side for myself as well, I'd been a mother for years and now it was like a new beginning, I was now allowed to be a kid and have a life of my own. I then realized that I would no longer have to change Jayvon's poopy diapers and no longer have to walk around for hours searching for Mitchell. But I also realized that I would no longer get to watch cartoons every Saturday morning with Jayvon or no longer have my pretend track team and street races with Mitchell, and I felt sad that so many great memories would be left behind, but happy that I would now be able to be a child instead of a parent.

Although on May 4, 1999 Kelly was now my new mom, I wasn't able to move into her home until a week later. Kelly and her boyfriend Bryan were two twenty-four year old college students about to move into their first home together, and before I was allowed to move in they had to make sure that their home met the state of Minnesota requirements. So, I was sent to live in a foster home with the Wilson's for a week until the house was finished. I didn't think that living with Kelly would be a problem at all seeing that I had known her almost a year, but Bryan, that was a different story. I had only met him once before and it was briefly, so I was already aware that moving into their home would be a little strange.

The week that I spent at the Wilson's went by extremely fast; besides going to school I spent the rest of my time in the house. Margi ordered the Wilson's as well as the Hall's to keep a close eye on my brothers and I because Egg had gotten out of jail the week before and decided to go around town telling people that she was going to have some people from Chicago, IL kidnap my brothers and I. Once I heard the fairy tale story that she was telling everyone I thought I was going to die from laughing so hard. I knew Egg was speaking nonsense simply because if no one was there to help us when we lived in Illinois in 1997, what's the chances of anyone coming to Minnesota to kidnap us and risk being thrown in jail. Slim to none. I found it extremely interesting how all of a sudden Egg wanted to play a important role in our lives now that we no longer lived with her, when just two weeks earlier she could have gave a rat's ass less where we were at, what we were doing, and who we were with. I guess you never miss what you have until it's gone.

Chapter 6
My New Life, Family, and Friends

Saturday May 15th was the day that I moved in with my new family. The house that we were going to be living in was the home in which Bryan had grown up in. The home belonged to Bryan's mom Tracy. It was a huge two story home that sat on top of a hill that over looked Highway 61 as well as both the big and small lakes. Kelly, Bryan, and I were to live upstairs, while his mother Tracy and her boyfriend Greg stayed down stairs. Tracy had been married years earlier but lost her husband Steve to cancer, in addition to this she had also lost her youngest son Peter in a fire that occurred before Steve was even diagnosed with cancer.

At the time when I met Tracy she was now a strong, independent women, as well as a mother of seven children. This included six boys and one girl. The first day that I arrived at the house I met more than half of Bryan siblings. I remember pulling up to the house and seeing kids running around in the yard. As soon as we pulled into the drive Bryan's family greeted us right away. All of his family members as well as their kids came over and introduced themselves. I did the same and then we proceeded to carry all of my belongings upstairs to my new bedroom.

Once inside, I began to set up my bedroom but tried not to get too settled in, because afterall I was only in temporary foster care until the county found a new home for me to live in. After I was done setting up my room I ate dinner with Kelly and Bryan and then I went to go and hang out with my friend Kenyon and her three girlfriends Nichole, Melissa, and Naomi.

Keyona was a friend that I had met back in seventh grade. I also used to date her brother Patrick at that time, but it was nothing serious, I was in seventh grade he was in eight and we decided that we were boyfriend and girlfriend. By now I was fourteen and dating a boy by the name of Daniel. Daniel was a boy that I had a crush on for most of my eight grade school year, and at a school dance I finally talked to him and now we were dating. I was now going out with Daniel, who was also my ex boyfriend Patrick's best friend. But it was no big deal; Patrick had a new girlfriend as well.

Now the way that I met Nichole, Melissa, and Naomi is a totally different story. Daniel and I had been dating for only a couple of weeks when I began to notice that he talked about sex a lot. Once he had mentioned something about how he liked girls to do sexual favors for him. I then told Daniel that I didn't do that kind of stuff and that if he wanted that done that he would have to go elsewhere. And that's when Nichole, Melissa, and Naomi come into play. When I told Daniel that he would have to go elsewhere and receive sexual favors from another girl, he chose to go in the direction of these three girls. At that point in time, it became very clear to me that Daniel wasn't boyfriend material and we both decided to call it quits.

Keyona was now one of my closest friends because she lived close by my new house, and I could no longer hang out with my old friends because Kelly and Bryan didn't like me hanging out around my old house. Kelly and Bryan had made up their minds that they were going to turn me into a better kid and they didn't want anything or anyone interfering. I remember that Kelly would always tell me "I just wish I could've gotten a hold of you when you were younger". She didn't have to say anything more, because I knew exactly where she was going. It's easy to have an impact on someone life when they're a child, but not as easy when their fourteen simply because at this age, they're already set in your ways.

Friday May 21st was the day that I was introduced to Kelly's side of the family. This would include: Kelly's parents Harry and Sally, as well as her younger brother, older sister and her two teenage nieces. May 21st was a special day because it was the day that Kelly graduated from college. So, on this day, both Kelly and Bryan's family came together and helped celebrate her great achievement. We all hung out at and ate pizza at a local restaurant that was built on land that stood in front of the Mississippi river. I didn't like hanging out with Kelly, Bryan, or their families for the longest time because I would always feel like an outcast or burden on them. So after we were done celebrating I went over to Keyona's house.

I visited Keyona's house all the time, one might even say that I practically lived there. This particular night I didn't know how long I would be hanging out with my new family so I told Keyona that I would stop by once we were done. I wasn't sure if she'd even be home, but to my surprise she was. Kelly and Bryan dropped me off and told me that they'd be back to pick me up at 10pm and I went inside the house. Once inside Keyona told me that I was just in time because she had just called a cab and that she was on her way to Nichole's house and that I could come with her. Nichole's house! I must admit that I was a little shocked once she told me where she was going. Because the first thing that popped in my mind was Daniel. He and I were no longer together, but with that in mind I knew that there were still harsh feelings between Nichole and I as well as Melissa and Naomi. Although I didn't know Nichole, I still told Keyona that I would go with her over to Nichole's house because I didn't have any harsh feeling towards her.

As soon as Keyona and I arrived to Nichole's house, there on the front steps sat Nichole, Melissa, and Naomi, and all three of them with a cigarettes in their hands. You could tell by the looks on their faces that they were surprised to see me; seeing that Keyona didn't tell them that I was coming over. I immediately got an adrenaline rush, I only came over to talk, but in the back of my mind I kept thinking what if they don't want to talk. I was both aware that a fight might break out, and prepared if one was to occur. I was fully aware that if there were to be a fight that it would be between Nichole and I because everyone knew that both Melissa and Naomi were afraid of their own shadows.

As Keyona and I walked towards the house, they just sat on the stairs watching us, and that's when Keyona said: "we ain't come over here to cause drama; she just wants to talk to you Nichole". I knew for sure that both Nichole and Melissa had fooled around with Daniel while we were dating, and I chose to talk to Nichole because I knew that she was the ringleader. Nichole agreed to talk to me and it was a total misunderstanding, Daniel had lied and told both Nichole and Melissa that we weren't together at the time that they messed around with him. I honestly could've cared less if Daniel told them that we weren't together or not simply because I gave him permission to go elsewhere because I refused give him what he wanted. But in the end once he started abusing his privilege I decided to cut him loose. I was extremely pleased with the conversation that Nichole and I had simply because I've never been the type to fight over a guy and didn't want to start that day. It's pointless because boys will be boys.

It was now the summer of 1999, and Nichole was now my new best friend. I no longer hung out at Keyona's house because I was always with Nichole, Melissa, and Naomi. I remember that one day I was visiting Nichole and I was sitting on her bed flipping through her yearbook and I came across a picture of me with the word "BITCH" written on it in big red capitol letters. I then turned to Nichole and asked her what was that all about. That's when she told me: "oh, I wrote that back when the whole Daniel thing was going on because I thought you were mean and that you didn't like me. But it doesn't matter now because we're friends"! She was right, that was all in the past, plus why would I get pissed when I already knew that I said the exact same thing about her before we met.

The summer of 1999 went by fast. My new friends and I spent most of our time getting drunk, having sex, and hanging out at the east end recreation center. I was fourteen years old when I got drunk for the first time. It would have been difficult for me to get drunk before the age of fourteen seeing that I was busy raising my brothers. But now I was free to do as I pleased. I remember that I'd get drunk in the early afternoon so I wouldn't still be drunk when Kelly and Bryan came to pick me up at 10pm. They weren't used to the whole parent thing, but it wouldn't be long before they got the hang of it.

I must admit that peer pressure played a major role in me starting to drink. I honestly started to drink because everyone else was doing it and seemed to be enjoying themselves, so I wanted to do the same. But sex, now that's a different story, I choose to have sex on my own. At the age of fourteen, no one pressured me into having sex with them. I just did it. I really don't understand why I was having sex at the age of fourteen But if I could turn back the hands of time I would have waited until I was at least eighteen I say this simply because between the ages of fourteen and seventeen, sex was just sex, to me. I got absolutely nothing out of it! I had sex most of the time because I was bored and there was nothing else to do. I'd have sex with a guy and think nothing of it, because it meant nothing to me. And that's what scared me the most, that and the fact that I couldn't figure out why I was doing it.

The east end recreation center was the place where, as Kelly and Bryan would say, all the local "pukes" and "shit-heads" hung out. And at the age of fourteen, I must admit that I did hang out with both. My girlfriends and I would go to the east end rec everyday to shot some pool, play games, and of course to watch the boys play basketball. This is where I met Adam. I asked Nichole if she knew who he was and she told me that Naomi knew him and said that he was a nice guy, but that she didn't want to date him because he was White.

It was kind of funny because Nichole, Melissa and Naomi were all White, but they only liked Black men. And of course I was the Black girl that loved White men. So, Naomi gave me Adam's number, I called him up and to my surprise he knew who I was. Adam told me that he used to always see me riding my bike past his house. In addition to this, Adam lived close by my house. He lived below the hill that I lived on in a house right next to the big lake. We seemed to hit it off pretty well, regardless of our three-year age difference. Adam and I would only date each other for a couple of weeks, but would remain friends for years to come.

It was now the end of August and the summer was quickly coming to an end. But my freshmen school year wasn't about to start without me finding out the real reason why my brothers and I were separated when Egg was sent to prison. I don't exactly remember how the topic was even brought up. But one day Kelly and I had been talking about the living situation of my brothers and I. It was at this point that Kelly told me that she had been keeping a secret from me, and now, she felt that I needed to know the truth. Kelly told me that both she and Margi had lied to me just months before when they told me that the reason why I wasn't able to live with my brothers was because Suzanne and Robert were only licensed to have three kids at the time. It was all a lie.

The only truth to this story was that at that point of time the Hill's were only licensed to have three kids at a time. But the rest of the story was nothing but Bullshit. Kelly told me that the real reason why I wasn't able to go and live with my brothers was because both Suzanne and Robert didn't want me to live with them. She also told me that the Hill's had planned all along to adopt my brothers the day that they found out that Egg was being sent to prison. I believe to this day that they didn't want me living in the same household because of the simple fact that I would be too much of a reminder of my brother's past. Not to mention the fact that I would somehow intervene with their plans to retrain as well as reinvent my brothers.

I must admit that when Kelly told me this I wasn't at all surprised. I knew that there was something that I didn't like about Suzanne Hill from the very first day I met her. Now it all made sense to me why I felt such a strange vibe when I was around her. But finding out that Margi had lied to me as well, now that hurt the most. Margi and I had built such a great relationship with each other and now I felt betrayed. I didn't understand how Margi, the women that didn't think twice about telling anyone how she truly felt, wasn't women enough to tell a fourteen year old girl why she was being taken away from the only family she had known. This is something that I know that Margi never forgave herself for either. This is why I believed she spent years showering me gifts. I know that Margi was just doing what she felt was the right thing to do. But why did I have to be the one to suffer for Egg's mistake.

Kelly told me that the only reason why she didn't tell me earlier was because she was trying to protect my feelings, but that she could no longer let me go on living a lie. I respect Kelly very much for telling me this because I realized that she could have chosen to continue to let me live a lie like everyone else was, but she didn't. This is a secret that I would carry for years, and never once showing any signs that I knew the truth. This would mean that whenever I was to be around Margi, Suzanne, or Robert that I would have to put a smile on my face and pretend like everything was great. This is a secret that I would keep to myself for years and for one reason only. The sake of my brothers, I didn't want them to know that the life that they were living was a lie as well. This is a secret that I would keep to myself, a secret that would go unknown for many years until now.

There's no enough words in the world to express how truly thankful I am for the family that I am apart of today. But I often wonder how different my life might've been if my brothers and I weren't separated.

Chapter 7
Rough Beginning, Smooth Ending

It was September 1999 and I was now entering High School. I started off the school as a troublemaker with a major attitude as well as anger problem. My first two weeks in high school I got grounded for shoplifting from Target with Nichole and Melissa. I got caught trying to steal a fake belly button ring and a tube of lipstick, while Nichole and Melissa got caught trying to steal all sort of make up, body spray, and a bunch of other stuff. The funny thing about the whole situation is that all three of us had to buy the items that we were trying to steal. We just wanted to see if we could get away with it, and of course we didn't succeed. I wasn't scared that I had gotten caught shoplifting at Target, but I was extremely afraid of what Kelly and Bryan would think or me as well as what they would say to me once I got home.

The first thought that came to my mind had something to do with me running away because I just knew that Kelly and Bryan were about to kick me out and I didn't want to be put in another foster home. The security guard that caught us shoplifting made each one of us dial our phone numbers and then talked to our parents and told them that we had been caught and that they needed to come and pick us up. Melissa was lucky; her parents were out of town and her older sister Sarah came to pick her up. Not that any of that would matter because neither Nichole nor Melissa got in trouble for shoplifting. But you can best believe that I did.

I was the first one that got to leave because I lived less than five minutes away, and Kelly came in a hurry. We both sat in silence the entire car ride home, once we arrived home she told me to go to my room and that we would talk about what I had done once Bryan got home from work. I was so ashamed about what I had done that I couldn't even look her in the face as she was speaking to me, but once I did, I wished that I hadn't because all I saw was the look of disappointment. I sat in my room for hours thinking to myself "how could you be so stupid Timesha, here you have these two wonderful people who welcome you into their home as well as their lives. And this is how you thank them, by going out and getting caught shoplifting".

Once Bryan got home from work, he and Kelly both called me out into the living room and told me that they were angry with me for shoplifting, but most of all they were very disappointed with me. They also told me that they felt like they weren't doing a good job raising me if I felt the need to go out and shoplift. I must admit that them telling me that they felt that they weren't been good parents hurt me a lot, simply because me shoplifting had nothing to do with them being bad parents. So, I got grounded and had to stay in the house for two weeks. I didn't mind it though, that just met that I would be less likely to get into any trouble for the next two weeks. But that wouldn't be the case.

Four days away from not being grounded anymore, I got in trouble again. This time I felt that I had done nothing wrong. Weeks before I had got caught shoplifting I met a boy by the name of Freddy at the East End rec. Freddy was in eleventh grade and we had been talking to each other at school as well as over the phone for weeks, and even though I was grounded Freddy said that he still wanted me to be his girlfriend and I agreed. Freddy had mentioned to me that he had an ex-girlfriend by the name of Maria that was still in love with him but I didn't think anything of it. I soon learned that the girl that he was talking about was the same Maria that was living in the foster home as my brothers.

Maria, as well as me not being able to control my anger, is what would caused me to get grounded all over again. On this particular day, I arrived to school and I had at least seven different people come up to me and tell me that Maria was running around school with a clipped out news paper article about Egg going to prison and my brothers and I being put into foster care. I couldn't believe what I was hearing, and I knew right then and there that someone had to teach this girl a lesson, and that someone was me. I consider myself to be a very honest person, you ask me any question about my personal life and I will give you an honest answer. But the one thing that I don't like is people who talk about me behind my back and then when they see me, have the nerve to come up to and try talking to me with a smile on their face.

This is exactly what Maria did every time we came in contact with each other, except for this particular day. I caught her in the act; she was standing by some girl that I didn't even know with the newspaper article in her hand. Melissa and I watched her from a distance. I let her have her fun because I knew that she was about to suffer the consequences for sticking her nose where it didn't belong. Once Maria was done having her fun bad mouthing me as well as my family, Melissa and I proceeded to walk towards her. I must have had a pissed off look on my face because as soon as Maria saw me, her look happiness was replaced by fear. I walked faster towards her and said "Maria can I please talk to you"? And just as she tried running away from me I grabbed her by the back of her neck, turned her towards me and punched her in her face. From that point on everything else was a blur.

I could've been in school for more than an hour that day, and now I was sitting in the principal's office. It was at this point that I realized that I was in trouble, but I was more than ready to take responsibility for my actions. The principal told me that he totally understood way I had reacted the way I did, but that it was the school policy and that he still had to suspend me from school for five days. Once again I sat in a chair looking stupid as someone called my house to tell Kelly and Bryan that I was in trouble once again.

Kelly arrived shortly, and drove me home and told me that she had to go back to work and that we would talk about what I had happen once she got home. So, once again I was grounded, but it wasn't because of me getting into a fight with Maria. It was because I had not followed the rules to being on probation, which meant no fighting. My probation officer sided with me just as everyone else did, but still said that he had to put me on house arrest for one week. House arrest wasn't as bad as it sounds, I didn't have a electronic bracelet around my ankle or anything like that, it just meant that I couldn't leave the house if I wasn't going to school or with Kelly or Bryan.

A few weeks, later Maria called my house and apologized for what she had done and I did the same. She then told me "it was dumb for us to fight over Freddy anyway". That's when I made it very clear to her that I didn't fight her over Freddy. I fought her simply because I didn't appreciate her trying to embarrass me in front of my peers. I told her that none of that mattered any way because it was all in the past and plus Freddy and I weren't together anymore. She asked me what had happen and I told her that he had cheated on me.

Freddy and I had been dating each other for about a month, and doing this time I would go and visit him in Houston, MN on the weekends. But there was one particular weekend that I couldn't go, so he found another girl that was willing to spend the weekend with. I remember that it was a Sunday night that Nichole called me up and told me that a girl by the name of May who was in eighth grade had spent the weekend with Freddy and that they had sex with each other. I knew that it was true right away. I decided right then and there that I didn't want to go out with Freddy anymore. So, me being the immature fourteen year old girl that I was, decided that I'd have Nichole three way Freddy on the phone and tell him that I didn't want to go out with him anymore.

My idea was to have Nichole talk to him and I would just listen, that was a big mistake. Nichole called and he answered the phone and she told him "I'm calling to tell you that Timesha doesn't want to go out with you anymore because you cheated on her". And Freddy's exact words back to her were "good, tell that Bitch that I really didn't like her anyway", and that was the end of the conversation. Afterwards, I thanked Nichole for calling Freddy for me; I then got off the phone and cried. I was crushed because that was the last thing that I had expected for Freddy to say. I thought that he would've at least tried denying it, but he didn't deny it nor did he show any remorse and that's what hurt me the most. None of this would matter because within a few weeks Freddy would learn that he and May were about to be parents at the age of seventeen and fourteen.

As I sat on my bed crying, Kelly came into my room and this was the first time in the five months that I had been living with them, that she had seen me cry. Although I turned away as soon as I saw her, she still knew that I was crying and rushed right over and sat next to me with both arms wrapped around me. She didn't even bother asking me why I was crying. In her eyes she could tell that I was hurt and needed her to comfort me. This is something that I had never experienced before; I had always been the one that would comfort others. This is when I saw how much Kelly truly loved me.

The year of 1999 had gone by fast and was quickly coming to an end. I was now doing much better in school. I was now on the varsity cheerleading team at my high school and I had also started taking a Jazz dance lessons outside of school at a local Arts Center. I had also met a really nice teacher by the name of Mr. Kruse. Mr. Kruse was my ninth grade American History teacher. I can honestly say that I have never met anyone like him. He is one of the most kind, gentle, and caring people that I have ever met in my entire life. Whenever I had any problems, whether they be school related or personal Mr. Kruse was always there to listen.

I also noticed that I was doing much better at home. No thanks to Beth, the physiatrist that my social worker Margi and my probation officer thought I should see. This would only last a couple of months simply because I'd just into her office once a week and listen to her talk, while never once talking back to her. I guess both Margi and my probation officer realized that it was a waste of money as well as time. I've said it once, and I'll say it again, "you can't force someone to get help, that's something that the individual who needs help must do on their own".

I remember the first time that I had ever been read a bedtime story and then tucked in was by Kelly, at the age of fourteen. And this is when I realized that I was opening up to both Kelly and Bryan, by allowing them to get close to me. These are two things that I had never done before in my life. I didn't bother opening up to people because I felt that they'd just betray you in the end by somehow using the information you told them against you. And I definitely didn't bother allowing anyone to get close to me because they'd just leave me in the end. But for some odd reason I no longer felt this way when it came to Kelly and Bryan. I was beginning to see them as my mom and dad instead of two people who we only ten years older than me.

Thanksgiving had gone by, and it was now Christmas. I was extremely excited that I would get to celebrate Christmas three times this year. The first Christmas that I got to celebrate was in Hutchinson, MN with Kelly's family. Christmas with Kelly's family was more of a calm as well as relaxing Christmas. We ate a lot of delicious food in the early afternoon. Then in the evening, we sat around in a circle opening gifts as we listened to Christmas music.

The second Christmas to be celebrated was the Christmas with my brothers. They came over to my house and we ate some snacks, exchanged gifts, and talked about what was going on in each other's lives. This was a special Christmas for both of my brothers because Suzanne and Robert had just adopted them. They were no longer Mitchell and Jayvon Williams. Instead, they were now Mitchell and Jacob Hill. That's right, the Hill's had changed Jayvon's name to Jacob. I must admit that I was angry with them changing his name, but at the same time I was happy for both of them.

The final Christmas to be celebrated was actually held the first weekend in January. This was the Christmas with Bryan's family. The reason why we celebrated Christmas so late is because Bryan's mother Tracy has a total of seven kids and it takes awhile to get them all together at the same time. Tracy's boyfriend Greg also had his three sons, and their wives come over as well. Bryan's Christmas was far from calm and relaxing. It was crazy, there had to be a least thirty people there, which is double the number of people that were at the Kelly's Christmas. All of Bryan's nieces and nephews were running around playing hide and seek. While everyone else either ate food, watched the football game on television, and played video games.

I enjoyed all three of these Christmas's, but I must admit that they were very different from all the other Christmas's that I'd ever celebrated in my entire life. I had grown very accustom everyone in my family getting drunk in the early afternoon, then by dark starting fights with each other and having the cops come over. So this was definitely a change for the good.

Chapter 8

It's Never as Bad as It Seems

The year of 2000 is the year that I would attempt to kill myself. It makes me sick to my stomach now when I sit back and think about it. I had gone through so many things and had never once thought about giving up until the April of 2000. And what exactly was it that caused me to think that my life wasn't worth living anymore? The fear of rejection, the fear that no one would want to be my friend or even want to speak to me again. Fear is what caused me to become a coward, and resulted in me almost overdosing off of Advil and Aspirin.

It all started in January of 2000 I had begun to hang out with an eighteen-year-old boy by the name of Justin. Justin was a guy that I had met in the summer of 1999 while hanging out with Nichole, Melissa, and Naomi. Everyone in the town knew who Justin was due to the fact that he was always getting into trouble. And of course at this point in time, if you got into a lot of trouble, then you were my type of guy.

Justin and I had begun hanging out with each other, as well as sleeping with each other. This had been going on for months; he would call my house all the time, as well as all hours of the night. He would sometimes use a fake name but I always knew it was him. I don't exactly remember how Kelly and Bryan found out about him. But I remember that there was this one incident that he called my house and Kelly answered the phone and said "he sounds pretty old, how old is he"? I didn't think that it was that big of a deal so I told her "he's eighteen". She then asked me "have you been hanging out with this boy"? I told her "yes". She then told me "you have no business hanging out with an eighteen year old".

Both Kelly and Bryan already knew that I was having sex, because Kelly had found my list of guys last summer. So when she asked me "are you having sex with this boy"? I didn't even bother lying, once again I told her "yes". I saw it in her face she was extremely upset. She then stood up and said, "I'm going to go and get Bryan"! And this is when I realized that I was in big trouble. As soon as Bryan walked into the living room where I was sitting, the first words out of his mouth were "what's this boy's name"? And that's when I went into an immediate panic. He had just asked me the one question that Kelly had forgot to ask.

I knew right then and there that the only reason he wanted me to give him a name was so that he could call the police department and report this "eighteen year old boy" for having sex with me. I knew that if I gave him Justin's name that Justin would be put in jail and that everyone in the entire town would hate me. Not to mention that all the guys would be afraid to talk to me. So I said "I'm not telling you his name"! Then Bryan told me "you can either tell me his name or tell it to the cops"! At this time I began to cry and stormed off to my room. Kelly ran after me and tried comforting me but I didn't want her to comfort me this time. I told her "don't touch me, I hate you, this is all your fault"! I saw the look of pain in her eyes as she left my room and shut the door behind her.

Bryan then opened up my bedroom door and told me "you have until tomorrow to decide what you're going to do". This is when I realized that I now had no point of living anymore. Everyone was going to hate me for getting Justin thrown in jail. Not to mention the fact that I would look like the girl that had sex with older men then cried rape. I made up my mind that night that I was going to kill myself. I attempted hanging myself from the ceiling fan in my bedroom, but we didn't have anything in the house that was strong enough to support my body weight. So I decided that I would take a lot of Advil and Aspirin then go to sleep. I know that I took fifteen Aspirin for sure and well over seventy Advil, and then I went to sleep.

To my surprise, I woke up the next morning. I couldn't understand it, I wanted to die, and I should've died. But I was still alive, so I knew from that day on that someone or something must have been watching over me that night to make sure that I woke up the next morning. I also realized that my survival meant that I had a purpose in life, as well as a reason to live. I then rolled out of bed, throw on the clothes that were nearest to me and stumbled downstairs and caught my bus to school. Once I arrived at school I saw Melissa and told her what had happened, and that I didn't feel well. She then told me that she'd leave school with me and that I could stay at her house for seven hours, until school was over with.

Between eight o'clock in the morning and three o'clock in the afternoon I vomited seventeen times. It was horrible; I wouldn't wish anything like this on my worst enemy. But it was the price that I had to pay, and it was well worth it because I had lived to see another day. That's when I realized that what I had done was stupid, as well as something that I would never do again, and that I really didn't want to die because I had so much more living to do.

I got home that day around three thirty in the afternoon and went straight to my room and worked on my homework that should have been due that day. Around six o'clock in the evening Kelly came into my room and told me that it was time for dinner. We ate dinner as a happy family and talked about how our day had been and not once was the topic of me having sex with an eighteen-year-old boy ever brought up. We never even spoke of this matter again. I believe it was because we had all done and said things that we really didn't mean the night before. And why dwell on the past.

The end of the school year was now coming to an end and this is when I found out that Mr. Kruse would not be returning. I was devastated, here I was standing in front of the one person who had helped me make it through my freshmen year in high school, and he was pretty much telling me good-bye. The one person that was always so willing to listen was now telling me that he was leaving. This was all happening because of stupid budget cuts, and the simply fact that Mr. Kruse was a new teacher. The one thing that I didn't understand is why the school district would rather cut new teachers, who didn't make nearly as much money as some of the teacher who had been there for years and would be soon retiring. But there was nothing that anyone could say or did it was final. Mr. Kruse would no longer be teaching at the High School.

It was now the summer of June of 2000, and this was the first time that my brothers and I went to visit Egg in prison. Egg had been in prison since October of 1999, and had been calling all three of us non-stop begging us ever since then, to come and visit her. So once we were out of school for the summer, we went to visit her in Shakopee, MN. This is where the women's prison was located. A women who worked for the County drove us to go and visit Egg. We must've driven past the prison at least four different times, simply because it looked more like college dorms than a prison.

Once inside it was nothing like I had expected. I assumed that everyone would be dressed in uniforms, but they weren't. They wore normal clothes, and they were even allowed to wear tennis shoes. They walked around freely, got to watch movies in the movie room, got to play basketball outside, and got to talk on the phone, as well as do each other hair in a salon. This wasn't a prison; it was more like a place where you got to do whatever you wanted exact you couldn't go any further than the basketball courtyard. And I sincerely believe that many of these women had a better life being locked up than they would if they were free. This way they at least had a warm place to sleep and food to eat.

The visit wasn't anything special. We sat in a room with Egg and a prison guard and answered all the questions that she preceded to ask us. The only problem was that she'd never let us finish giving her our answers because she'd always find some kind of way to tie herself into the story and the take over the conversation. Yep, she was still the same old Egg, always and will forever be inconsiderate of others. Throughout the visit she kept calling Jacob, by his old name "Jayvon" when she was fully aware that his name had been changed six months when the Hill's adopted both he and Mitchell.

We visited with Egg for two hours, but it felt like a lifetime. Both my brothers and I were more than happy to go back home. The funny thing is that none of us wanted to visit Egg to begin with, we just felt obligated to do so. But of course we couldn't get out of there without taking a picture with her and of listening to her famous line "look how grown up my babies are." Then she turned to the prison guard and said "don't I have some beautiful babies"? He nodded his head and smiled, then Egg gave all of us a hug and kiss, and we headed back to home.

The summer of 2000 is also when I got my first job. July 3, 2000 was the day that I started working at Burger King. I was sort of forced to go out and find a job. Margi my social worker, decided that she didn't want me sitting around doing nothing all summer, so she gave me the choice of either finding a job or being sent away for the summer to chop down trees somewhere up by Duluth, MN. It was the middle of summer and I defiantly knew that I didn't want to be standing outside all day long in scorching hot weather trying to chop down trees. So I went out and found myself a job. My first job would be working at Burger King. I enjoyed working at Burger King a lot. Although I only worked there eight months, I didn't feel bad leaving because I left on good terms with all the mangers. But the manger that I admired the most was Kris. Kris was a great manger as well as a fun person to work with, and someone that I still keep in contact with to this day. Working at Burger King was a great experience and I wouldn't trade for anything.

When August of 2000 came around my friends and I were in for a big surprise. This is the month that Nichole, Melissa, and I found out that our friend Naomi was pregnant. Naomi had been seeing a guy that she'd met a couple months back and now she was about to be a mother at the age of fifteen. It was kind of funny because we were all having sex and used to always joke around about who would be the first one to get pregnant, and we always figured that it would be Melissa because she was the one that always talked about babies. But we were all wrong, out of the four of us, Naomi would be the first to have a baby, and she would continue having babies from that point on.

It was now September and school was in progress all over again. I was now a sophomore and I must admit that I was filling a little bit down on my first day back to school. I was disappointed mainly because I knew that Mr. Kruse would not be returning to teach this school year. But at the same time I was excited that Nichole would be attending the same school as Melissa and I because she was now a freshmen. I arrived to school early and met up with Melissa and Nichole. We then sat down at a table that was located in the middle of the concourse and talked about what classes we were going to be taking this year.

There then came a point in time when I got up to walk over to the vending machine to buy a bag of potato chips, and who did I see standing in front of the school with his hands behind his back. It was Mr. Kruse; he was standing in front of some lockers wearing a grey suit. I walked over to Mr. Kruse and gave him a big hug and told him that it was nice to see him again. I asked him what he was doing back at the High school because he was one of the new teachers that distract had cut just three months earlier. This is when Mr. Kruse told me that he would no longer be teaching American History anymore because he was now the new Dean of Students. And it was at this point that I realized that Mr. Kruse wasn't going anywhere, because I knew that they had choosing the perfect man for the job.

For the next three years, Mr. Kruse would be the one to help guide me through my high school years. Whether they were good times or bad times, Mr. Kruse was always there, and never once, not even for a second turned his back on me. There were times when I honestly thought that I wouldn't make it through high school, but Mr. Kruse was always there to boost me up. I remember when there was this one incident involving a huge fight at my school. The fight was race related, a group of Black kids had gotten into a fight with a group of White kids and it was complete mayhem. The police were even called to our school.

The fight took place before eight thirty, which is the time when school started. I wasn't in school when the fight occurred, but I still heard about what had happened because it was the talk of our school. I remember that I was sitting in my first hour class and the phone rang and the teacher answered it. The teacher then walked over to me and said "Timesha, Mr. Kruse needs to speak to you downstairs in his office". I obvious knew that I had done nothing wrong, so I was kind of curious as to why he would need to speak with me. Once I was downstairs in Mr. Kruse's office he welcomed me, asked me to have a sit and preceded to talk to me about the fight that had just occurred earlier that morning.

Mr. Kruse then asked me if anyone had done or said anything to offend me, and I told him "no". Mr. Kruse's exact words to me with tears in his eyes were "Timesha I'm asking you this because if anyone were to say anything or to do anything to harm you in any way at all, I would just lose all self control. I care about you a lot and think you're a wonderful student and the last thing that I would want is for you to get hurt". As he spoke to me I sat there with tears in my eyes as well and listened to him speak. It was at this point that I realized how much Mr. Kruse truly cared for me and how much I truly cared for him.

Chapter 9
My Highs and Lows of 2001

As January 2001 quickly approached I was still in tenth grade, and this is when I smoked marijuana for the first time. I smoked it for the first time when I was hanging out with Nichole and some of her girlfriends. From that day on, I started smoking weed non-stop. I know that you can't get addicted to weed, but I do know that I was very dependent on weed for many years. I can honestly say that there was a time when I smoked weed at least five out of the seven days in a week. It got to the point where I'd go to school early just so I could stand outside and get high before school started. After school was the same, as soon as school got out at three o'clock I'd hurry up and get high then still somehow manage to make it to work by three fifteen.

The reason why I chose to smoke weed, one again was because my friends were doing it, plus it was something that I always wanted to try. Once I did it for the first time I really liked it. Unlike alcohol, you can smoke as much weed as you want, have a fun time while doing so, and still wake up in the morning feeling great. I don't know why but it seemed like everything was so much better when I was high. Whether it be how relaxed my body felt, how good the food that I would normally never eat taste, having sex, the ability to laugh when nothing was even funny, and the ability to feel as if I was flying by simply riding a bike or rollerblading, and most of all the ability to sleep like I'd never slept before.

Marijuana would be one of my new best friends, as well as my drug of choice for the rest of my high school years. While many kids that I would soon graduate with were out getting drunk or snorting lines of cocaine, I was getting high. I would have to say that I probably got drunk a total of four times while in high school, and never once snorted anything. The one and only reason why I never came home drunk while in high school was because Kelly would always be waiting for me to walk through the front door to ask me how my night went. The reason behind not snorting cocaine was because I had already seen first hand with my own family, how much it could truly ruin someone's life. So, I got as high as I could, came home paranoid, ate so food, made up some excuse about my eyes being red because my contacts were acting up, and then were to bed. This would be my nightly routine for years to come.

March 12, 2001 was the day that I started working at my new job at a local grocery store. March 12, 2001 was also the day that Bryan got his title of being a Police officer. He was extremely excited because he had applied to many police departments in other towns, and there was even talk about us having to move to another town if he was to be hired else where. But there would be no need for us to relocate because he was offered a position in his hometown.

I had the job at the grocery store in February of 2001, but the store manager told me that I had to wait until I turned sixteen. This was by far the best job that I have ever had in my entire life, and the person to thank was Margi because she was the one that got me the job. Both Margi and the store manager had been friends for years, so the job was pretty much just giving to me. I can honestly say that I don't think that I would have been hired if it weren't for Margi. And, now that she had gotten me the job, I had to hold up my end of the bargain by proving that I was worthy of it.

The grocery store is one of the best jobs that I have ever worked at in my life. Overall, I would have to say that everyone who works there is like a big family. This is the one and only job that actually looked forward to going to. Why? Because I loved everything about it, whether it was the customers, my follow employees, the managers, the owner, scanning grocery items, bagging groceries, frying chicken in the deli, or even cleaning bathrooms, I enjoyed it all. It was a great experience, and I wouldn't trade it for anything else in the world. Because there's nothing better than loving what you do.

April 15, 2001 is the day that I would meet the famous rapper known as Nelly. Each year Winona State University has a spring concert, where they pay a famous singer to come and perform at the college. This particular year it was kind of funny because there were many people saying that it was going to be the pop singer Nelly Furtado who sang, "I'm like a bird", while others were saying that it was going to be the rapper Nelly who sang "Country Grammar". Nichole and I just knew that it was Nelly the rapper so we went and bought our fifteen-dollar tickets.

The concert was general admission and started at eight o'clock in the evening. So, Nichole and I got there a little before six o'clock, and managed to sneak our way to the front of the line. While standing outside we say Fredro Starr who is the singing in a rap group called Onyx. He is also known as a bad guy named Maliki in "Save the last dance" which starred Julia Stiles and Sean Patrick Thomas. Once we saw him, we knew that we had indeed bought tickets to see Nelly the rapper. The doors opened around seven o'clock, and Nichole and I were the first two people inside.

We stood in the very front row and waited for an hour for the show to begin. Once the show began we got a great view of all of the rappers on stage, as well as great sound effects seeing that the speakers were located right next to us. We watched and listened to Onyx, the St. Lunatics, and even the rapper Royce Da 5'9 who raps in Willa Ford's "I wanna be bad" was there. But Nelly was the last one to come on stage. Ashley and I were right in front, and throughout the show we both noticed that Kejuan, a member from the St. Lunatics kept staring at us. At the time we didn't know who he was staring at, but we would find out shortly.

There then came a point in time during the concert when Nelly told the crowd that he had never been to Winona before and that he needed someone to come take a ride with him as well as show him around town. And everyone including Nichole and I went crazy, we starting jumping up and down screaming with our hands in the air. Murphy Lee, from the St. Lunatics picked a girl from the middle of the crowd, and then Kejuan looked right down at me and pulled me onto the stage. I was shocked, I couldn't believe that I had just been picked to go on stage and that I was about to go for a ride with Nelly. Little did I know that the ride wouldn't even involve me leaving the building

Once on the stage I looked out into the crowd and all I saw was thick layers of smoke from all the weed smoking that had been going on every since the concert started. I then looked to my right hand side and saw three chairs sitting in the middle of the stage. Nelly then asked the girl and I what our names were and if we wanted to go for a ride with him. We told him our names and or course we said that we wanted to go for a ride with him. That's when Nelly's "Ride wit' me" song came on, and we both got to sit next to Nelly in the middle of the stage, as he sang "Ride wit' me".

It was crazy because any other person would have been in shock that Nelly was sitting right next to them singing. But I wasn't, I more shocked by all the jewelry he had on. The lights just shined in all different colors off of his diamond earrings as well as his platinum chains, watches, and bracelets. After the song Nelly signed a poster as well as a pink bandanna for me. After the concert Nelly stood outside in the pouring rain and signed posters, shirts, as well as varies body parts. I got my shirt signed, while Nichole got her shirt as well as a poster signed. I remember that a girl was pushing and screaming asking Nelly to sign her poster as he was already singing someone else's. Nelly replied to her "I will in one moment sweetheart". And it was then that I realized how much Nelly truly cared for his fans, he cared enough that he was willing to stand outside in the pouring rain just to make sure that everyone got an autograph.

May 12, 2001 was the day that my mom Kelly and my dad Bryan got married. We were now officially a family: mom, dad, and daughter. The wedding as well as the reception had a wonderful turn out, minus the fact that I got a little drunk and threaten to "beat the girl's ass" that told my mom that I was drinking. I had been drinking fuzzy navels all night long and then when I was confronted, I let the alcohol take over. This was the first time that I had ever used profanity towards my mom. Although I wasn't referring to her, I was still using words that she had never heard me use before. Although my mom told me that I didn't ruin her wedding, deep down inside I still feel that I did ruin their special day.

By the time summer came around, it seemed like everyone was pregnant. My mom had gotten pregnant shortly after her wedding, Naomi already had a baby boy and was also carrying her second child, while Melissa was pregnant and would soon be the mother of a little girl. Nichole and I were the only two that weren't having babies yet. Nichole and I were still extremely close but we didn't hang out as much because I now had a new best friend by the name of Angela.

Angela and I had been on the same cheerleading squad back in 1999, and Angela lived right up the street from our new home that we moved into just before my mom and dad got married. Angela was now my new best friend, we were both sixteen and going into the eleventh grade, we did everything together. We both shared the love for Chinese food, our favorite singer was Aaliyah, we both ran two miles together everyday, we both loved to write poems, we both loved to smoke weed and then go rollerblading, and we even pretended like we were rapper for awhile. Her name was The WG (white girl) and mine was Big T.

Angela and I also both loved to dance, so we would seek out of our houses late at night and go dancing at a local club. The house that we lived in was a one and a half story home, so I'd climb the half story part and the jump down to the ground. I remember this one night when I was just about to jump down Angela told me to hurry up because a police officer was driving down the street. Just as I hit the ground the police officer had pulled in front of my house and shut his lights off. Angela and I hide behind a trashcan and waited to see what was going to happen next.

The driver door swung open and out came my dad. I just about died, because both Angela and I knew that he had to have seen me jump off the roof. He went inside the house and we both assumed that he was going to check and see if I was in my bedroom or not. A couple of minutes later we heard him and my mom talking outside on our deck, then his walkie-talkie went off. It was at this point that Angela and I both decided that we'd better make a run for it and that I would just suffer the consequences in the morning.

I was around one thirty in the morning and the nightclub was close when Angela and I met four guys that asked us if we wanted to come and party with them. I honestly don't even remember their names. But,

Angela and I both decided that it sounded like a good idea, I then turned to Angela and said "I might as well have fun tonight because I'm about to be grounded first thing tomorrow for sneaking out". I've never been so paranoid in my entire life; I ducked behind the nearest object every time I saw a car coming in fear that it might be my dad. I stayed slouched down the entire car ride to these guys house in fear that my dad might drive by and see me. And I even shut my cell phone off in fear that my dad might call and ask me where I was.

Once we arrived to this apartment that was located on the east end of town, we learned that these guys didn't even live there. A girl by the name of Michelle lived there and was just allowing them to stay with her simply because they were supplying her with free drugs. We stayed there for hours while everyone got drunk, smoked weed, snorted lines of cocaine, and even did some whip it's. Angela and I just smoked weed and drank some beers. This would be the night that I would have my first and only one night-stand. I got drunk and high then had sex with a guy that I had just met then never seen him again. He told me that his name was Anthony, but he could've made it up.

I knew that my dad worked the eleven at night to seven in the morning shift, so I got home around six thirty in the morning and went to sleep. I woke up in the late after noon feeling hung over as well as dirty for all the things that I had done just hours before. I took a shower then went downstairs and hung out with my mom, and never once did she mention anything about me sneaking out. This wasn't the first time that I had snuck out nor would it be the last. But in due time my parents would find out about my many late night creeps.

Chapter 10

I Don't Know What's Come over Me

By the time the year 2002 came around I was in the eleventh grade as well as a full bloomed pothead. Everything I did as well as everyone I knew somehow had something to do with smoking marijuana. This was also the year that my grades would suffer a great deal simply because I choose to get high all the time instead of study. I was doing so bad in school that I couldn't even maintain a C average, which is what I needed if I didn't want to get grounded. I wasn't able to maintain a C average so I had no choice but to resort to lying and cheating. I couldn't get grounded, because then I wouldn't be able to smoke weed. So lied to my high school and told them that I no longer lived with my parents and gave them a new address to mail all of my school information to.

Next, I had to start making my own report cards then bringing them home. This is what I spent most of my junior year in high school doing as well as hanging out with my four new pot smoking buddies: Amy, Simone, Jamie, and Monica.

Amy and I had been working together at the grocery store for over a year. Simone and I started hanging out simply because both our mom's were family counselor's that worked together. Jamie and Simone played soccer together and were close friends. Monica was the basketball player as well as friends with everyone. And of course I did many different things when it came to getting high with these four individuals.

Amy and I would go to work as well as football and basketball games high. Simone, Jamie, Monica, and I would party and get high at or just simply drive around or get high down by the lake. I'd have to say that to a certain degree us smoking pot was a good thing consider that fact that the majority of kids that we went to high school with had already graduated to snorting lines, eating mushrooms, and popping pills! But, we were all too scared to try any of that. Overall, we were just your typical high school kids experimenting with marijuana.

In a weird way it was kind of like I was living a double life. My mom and dad both said that I needed to find some new friends, so I did. They didn't like me hanging out with Nichole, Melissa, and Naomi because they got into a lot of trouble and were also popping babies out like crazy, so my parents viewed them as hoodlums. But they liked my new friends a lot. Amy, Simone, Jamie, and Monica were good girls in my parent's eyes, for two reasons: 1) they didn't get into trouble and 2) most of all they were preppy. Although these were my new friends and I liked them a lot, I still wasn't just going to completely stop talking to my old friends because they were the only ones who truly knew the real Timesha.

The reason that I say it was kind of like I was living a double life is because I hung out with Amy, Simone, Jamie, and Monica by day. But by night, I was hanging out with Nichole and Melissa. Naomi really didn't hang out with us once she had her son and had gotten pregnant again. But, once again I had begun to sneak of my bedroom window on a nightly basis, and this time it wasn't to go dancing at the nightclub. Nichole, Melissa and I had befriended seven drug dealers from Chicago, IL. We'd party with them all night long. I had also started hanging out with my old drug dealer friends Fallon and Tamara again. I had known these girls since I was thirteen but had lost contact with once my brothers and I went into foster care. They both had kids now but they were still the same as I had remembered them.

I was getting out of control, I had begun sneaking out of my bedroom window at least five out of the seven days in a week, and three of which were school nights. The reasoning behind my sneaking out was simple, I wanted to get drunk and smoke weed. Both of these things happened each night that I snuck out of my house. I'd have to be home by ten o'clock, which was fine because by the time eleven o' clock rolled around I was out partying again.

I'd usually leave my house around eleven or eleven thirty and return home around six or six thirty in the morning. My dad came home at seven and I had to make sure that I was home before then. I'd spend all night getting drunk and high, but I still managed to make it to school everyday. The only reason why I believe my friends and I hung out with these guys was because they supplied use with free alcohol and weed. While other people might say that the only reason that these guys hung out with us was because we were having sex with them, but the way I see it is that the whole sex thing works both ways.

I believe that I was sixteen at the time that I had sex with Brad, who was one of the seven drug dealers. Brad was twenty-seven, but that didn't bother me at all because I loved older men, and so did all my friends. We parted like rock stars for two months straight and then it all came to an end one morning when the Police Department did a pre-dawn raid on our party house. It's kind of funny because there would be at least fifteen to twenty people in the house at a time partying into the early morning, but on the day that that police raided the house there were only seven people there, all of which were the drug dealers who lived there.

I guess it was a good thing that I didn't go over to Brad's house that night considering the fact that my dad was one of the many officers that participated in the drug bust. It amazes me that my friends and I weren't at the house the day that it was raided because it happened at five thirty in the morning on a weekday and we were always there. But then again, if I was there I was have had a lot of explaining to do considering the fact that at five thirty in the morning on a weekday I'm suppose to be at home sleeping. I guess it was luck, because it always seems that I was so close to getting caught, and then whatever it is that I've done wrong just bypasses me.

After this incident I decided that I needed to change my lifestyle as soon as possible. Because I'd come so close to being caught to many times for doing stupid things that I had no business doing. I realized that if I was to get caught doing the things that I was doing as well as hanging out with the people that I was hanging out with, that my future would be ruined.

I would be viewed as a menace to society, but worst of all, my parents would be looked down on for not doing a good job raising me, and this is something that I wasn't about to allow happen. The last thing that I would want to do is have people look down on them because of the things that I chose to do. They'd done an excellent job raising me. And it would only be a matter of time before I made everyone aware of this.

It was now spring and I was two months away from being done with my junior year in high school, but I still decided that I would at least try to bring my G.P.A up a little. It's kind of sad that I was down to my last two months in school, and I was just now beginning to take school seriously. By this time I was still smoking weed, but I was no longer sneaking out of the house to get drunk, making fake report cards, and I even went back to school and gave the office my real address because my mom thought it was a little weird that she was no longer was receiving mail from my school. It was also around this same that Naomi was now the mother of two and Melissa had just giving birth to a little girl. But the most important birth of the year happened on April 5, 2002.

April 5, 2002 was the day that my parents Kelly and Bryan were giving a beautiful baby boy name Peter Michael. I thought it was very unique how his entire name has meaning behind it. His first name was giving to him in memory of my dad younger brother Peter, who died in a house fire when they were younger. And, his middle name Michael, was giving to him because it's the name of my mom's younger brother who she loves dearly.

Peter came as a surprise to all of us because he wasn't scheduled to arrive until the end of April, but instead he was born almost three weeks early. This fact alone would cause Peter to spend almost a month in the hospital trying to fight off a case of Jaundice. Peter's blood levels were extremely high and there was even a point in time that the doctors told my parents that he could possible be blind or mentally retarded. Needless to say, this was a very difficult time for my parents and I, as well as anyone that was close to us.

Both of my parents had taking a lot of time off from work and had been sleeping in the hospital for weeks to be by Peter's side. So, this meant that I was home alone for weeks, which would give me all the time in the world to do as I pleased. This time I wouldn't have to scale my roof top I could just simply walk right out the front door or invite anyone I wanted to over to my house and do whatever my heart desired. But I didn't do either one, instead I stayed home and studied, cleaned the house and I even tried doing laundry for the first time at the age of seventeen. The clothes didn't quit turn out the way they should have. Instead I let them sit in the washer too long and they became mildewed. So from that day forth I left the whole laundry thing up to my mom.

I went to visit my parents and Peter a few times while they stayed in the hospital, but for the most part I just talked to them over the phone every night. The major reason why I didn't visit them as often as I should've while they were staying in the hospital is because I have a major problem when it comes to expressing how I truly feel. My parents were going through a lot of pain with Peter was sick, and so was I. I was worried about Sean because he was just a helpless baby with no idea as to what was going on. But I was even more worried my parents. It hurt me a lot to see them in as much pain as they were in. But it hurt me even more to know that there was absolutely nothing that I could do to take their pain away as they had always done for me.

So I did the only thing I could do, which was to behave myself and not get into any trouble because I knew that they were already under a lot of stress and the last thing they needed to deal with was me getting in to trouble. I remember that there was this one particular time that my mom came home from the hospital to get some things that her and my dad needed from the house. I remember that she had decided to do a load of laundry while she was home and I stood in the laundry room and talked to her as she sat on the floor sorting the dirty clothes into separate piles. As we proceeded to talk to each other about how proud she was of me for taking care of the house as well as behaving myself, she became very sad and started to cry.

Now, I'd seen her cry a thousand times before because she's a very emotional person. It could be the smallest thing from a movie we were watching to a commercial about saving trees and she'd start to cry. But this time there was actually meaning behind her crying. She was crying because her first child was in the hospital sick and she felt like it was her fault simply because he was born early, but she was also crying because she felt like she was neglecting me by not be home to be a good mother.

That's when I walked over to her, wrapped one arm around her and rubbed my other hand across the top of her head and told her "don't cry, because if you cry then you're going to make me cry". And then I started to cry. I had grown so accustom to her always being there to comfort me, and for the first time in my entire life I was the one comforting her. I then told her "don't worry about me I'm a big girl, I'll be fine, and so will Peter". And I was right, Peter recovered from Jaundice in no time, and we were now a family of four.

By the time October of 2002 came around Egg was done doing her time in the big house and was now being released from prison after serving three and a half years. She decided that she wasn't going to move back to town, which made everyone happy. Instead, Egg decided that she was going to live in St. Paul, MN, with a woman that she had met in prison. This didn't last long and Egg would continue to move from shelter to shelter for years. You'd think that she'd get out prison and at least try to better her life. But of course she didn't and she was still the same old Egg.

The only difference was that she walked into prison weighing one hundred and ten pounds and walked out weighing two hundred and ninety pounds. She came back to town and visited for about five days, and of course I hung out with her. Why? Because of guilt, she had lost all her legal rights of my brothers and I guess that I felt somewhat obligated to spend time with her. While she was in town she stayed with two different women by the names of Vera and Grace.

Vera was a woman that Egg had met back in 1997 when we first moved to town. At the time Vera worked at the battered women's shelter that Egg would frequently visit. Egg had never been a battered women and I know that Vera knew this as well, but like me she just felt somewhat obligated to talk to her. While, Grace was a woman that Egg had met back in 1998. They were long time drinking buddies, not to mention that Grace lived right next door to Egg's old boyfriend Richard. I hung out with Egg at least three different times, and all three times she was getting drunk. What can I say? Some people never change.

It was now December of 2002, and I was about to come face to face with my pass and it wasn't my choice either. This is the month that I would be talking to my brother Mitchell, who was now eleven on the phone. This would be the first time that I was forced to speak of an incident that I vowed never to speak of again. I don't remember the exact date but I do know that it was right before Christmas because I remember asking him what he wanted for Christmas. Whenever Mitchell and I would talk on the phone I would always ask him questions like how he was doing in school and things of that nature. But for some odd reason Mitchell would always ask me, "Do you remember that time when…"? I guess in a weird way Mitchell saw me as a connection to his previous life. Most of the time Mitchell's, "Do you remember that time when" would consist of us making fun of Egg for something stupid she'd done when we were younger. But this wasn't the case when it came to this particular conversation.

Mitchell's exact words to me were "do you remember that time when you saved my life when we first moved to Minnesota". And I broke down; I couldn't believe that that he actually remembered what happened. I told him "yes" as I slightly pulled the phone away from ear and started to cry. He proceeded to talk about what had happened that day by saying "well I just wanted to thank you for saving my life. Mom would've killed me if you hadn't been there to save me". That's when I told Michael to forget about it because it was all in the past and we were both with two wonderful families that loved us and that he didn't have to ever worry about anything like that happening again.

Chapter 11
Class of 2003

I'd had many rough times throughout my four years in high school, but my senior year was by far my best year in high school. This would be the year that I show everyone that I had overcome all obstacles in my life and that I was now ready to take on the world. No one, including myself could have expected all of the good things that were to come. Who ever said that good things come to those who wait, must've been referring to my senior year in high school. It seemed as if everything was too good to be true.

My senior year started out with me finally getting my driver's license. I'd had my drivers permit since I was fifteen and I really didn't care too much about driving because I was actually scared. But after I had to renew my permit on two different occasions, my parents told me that I'd had my permit for two years and it was time for me to get my license. So, my dad and I practiced driving for weeks because my mom said that she was too scared to get in the car with me. I was kind of funny because my dad would have me doing crazy things that any normal person wouldn't actually do while they were driving.

I remember that there was this one time that he made me parallel park between two semi trucks, now what's the likelihood of me ever having to parallel park between two semis. Or another time when he had me practice pulling into parking spaces. It was an empty lot and as I was driving he'd have me pull into random spots. Well one of the times that I pulled into the parking space I kind of ran over the white line. It was at this point that he turned to me and said "Timesha, you just failed your test". And my response was "what"? He then said, "You just ran over the white line which means that you just hit the car that was parked next to you". My next response was "there's no car there". Then he replied, "But what if there had been"?

So by the time September 24, 2002 rolled around I was walking into the Drivers Center to take my road test with a driving instructor. My mom went with me, and was scared to death that I'd be taking the test in her car. I remember that I was hardcore rocking out to my mom's Linkin Park cd. And I got extremely pumped. My road test instructor was an older man, he came over and inspected the car to make sure that it was safe to be on the road, and off we went.

We couldn't have been driving any longer than ten minutes. The instructor had me parallel park, which I successfully did and 90 degree park, with I totally screwed up and the only other words that came out of his mouth were: "make a right", "make a left", "switch to the other lane", and "head back to the Driving Center". So I was sure that I had failed as well as pissed him off. Once we were back at the Driving Center, we both hopped out of the car and he finished filling out my form, and told me that I had passed.

I walked upstairs to the waiting room that my mom was sitting in and told her that I didn't pass. She then gave me a weird looking because she knew that I wasn't telling the truth. I then told her that I had passed and we both went to get my picture taken and then I had to go to school. Once I arrived to school and walked through the doors I had people walking up to me saying "Congratulations Timesha"! And I was extremely puzzled because I had only told a handful of people that I was going to try and get my license that morning, not to mention that I had only had it for about twenty minutes and the only two people that knew were my mom and dad.

The first person that I saw that day was my best friend Amy, and she asked me if I had gotten my license and I told her yes and the she said "Good job. Oh yeah, I also want to congratulate you on being "Winhawk of the Week". I then looked at her and said "what, Winhawk of the week"? And she said, "yep you're the Winhawk of the Week, your picture is hanging up over there in that glass bulletin. Didn't you know"? Actually I didn't know, but I walked over to the glass bulletin and sure enough there I was. It was a picture of me and in big bold letter at the top of the paper it said "Timesha Mullins, Your Winhawk of the Week", and then it went into detail about my parents names, how many siblings I had, my favorite color, food, television show, as well as my hobbies.

September 24, 2002 is the day that I got my drivers license as well as the day that I became Winhawk of the Week. The Winhawk of the Week award is giving out weekly throughout the entire school year. It's sort of like a student of the week type of deal, but at our school it was called the Winhawk of the week because our school mascot was a "Hawk" and we like to "Win". So that's how the name "Winhawk" originated.

In order to be Winhawk of the week I believe that you have to be nominated by at least six teachers. And I actually found out that I was suppose to have been Winhawk of the Week my junior year but the school ran out of time and had to transfer it over to my senior year. This achievement would make me a star, because it was posted in the Daily News paper. This was a proud moment for both my parents and I. This was the first time that I'd been in the newspaper but it wouldn't be the last.

It was now November of 2002; I had always loved English class as well as writing poems, so I decided to enroll in a class called Creative Writing. There came a time in class when my teacher Mrs. Jones told the entire class that there was a company that was publishing a book of poems that were written by young creative writers. Mrs. Jones then told us that we could submit one of poems if we wanted to and that she would mail it for us. Mrs. Jones didn't hear from the company until sometime in December, and when she did it was good news.

The publishers of this company had chosen a few poems from our class that were to be published in their book. My poem that was titled "Remember" was one that had been chosen.

Remember

I don't exactly remember what the fight was about
But why would it matter seeing that I'm always wrong
I will never forget the way you walked out
How could one person have so much clout
But I finally built up my courage to be strong
I don't exactly remember what the fight was about
Our love I thought I'd never doubt
I still can't grasp the fact that you're gone
I will never forget the way you walked out
You'd never talk to me instead you'd shout
Saying it's my fault and that you're never wrong
I don't exactly remember what the fight was about
I try hard to block the bad memories out
But now it's to late because you're gone
I will never forget the way you walked out
Now I'm able to live with clout
Because you taught me how to be strong
I don't exactly remember what the fight was about
I will never forget the way you walked out

Remember, is a villanelle poem that consists of nineteen lines with one of the most beautiful rhyme scheme. This by far was the best poem that I had ever written in my entire life. So, there I was getting one of my greatest achievements published in a book. Once again my parents were extremely proud of me, and once again I received an award and was in the Daily News paper. My mom told me that the poem I wrote was very beautiful. She also has told me that she felt that it ties into my personal life. I disagreed by telling her "I completely made that poem up, so there's no way that it could possibly tie into my life". But deep down inside I knew she was right.

It was now Saturday, February 1, 2003, and our Winterfest dance would be the following Saturday on February 8, 2003. Amy and I both worked with a couple of students who were part of the student counsel committee. The members of this committee planed all of the school dances. They would find out on Friday who the twelve students to be nominated for the school year would be, while the rest of the school wouldn't find out until the following Monday. Amy and I had connections, so we'd know who was going to be on court by Friday as well. But this year was different, everyone seemed so secretive and none of the people that I knew that worked for the student counsel committee would tell me who was going to be on court. So I quit trying, after all the entire school would know in two days anyway.

It was now Monday February 3, 2003, everyone knew that on the Monday before a dance that it was "Dress up day" and Friday would be "Orange and Black day" which were our school colors. As for Tuesday, Wednesday, and Thursday, we'd find out once we got there on Monday. Needless to say, there were a lot of people dressed up including Amy and I. Amy and I always came to school early and sat around and talked to our friends. This particular day a mutual friend of ours by the name of Michelle came over and said "Congratulations Timesha for getting on court"!

I gave Michelle an odd look and glanced over at Amy, as she stood there with her mouth hanging open. I smiled at Amy and Michelle both. Amy then turned and punched Michelle in the arm and said, "she didn't know she was going to be on court dumb ass"! And Michelle replied, "Oh my God, I'm so sorry I though you already knew"! I told her that I knew now, and that it was okay because I was about to find out in about fifteen minutes anyway. Then it hit me, the reason why no one would tell me who was on court was because one of the twelve people was me.

It was now eight thirty in the morning and the twelve hundred students of my High School stormed into our school gym and sat anxiously as our Winterfest nominees were to be announced. The gym was divided into four separate sections, one for the freshmen, one for the sophomores, one for the juniors, and one for the seniors. I sat in the senior section with Simone, Jamie, Monica, and although Amy was only a junior she still sat with us. Plus Amy was my best friend, where ever I went, she went as well.

In order to made court you have to be a senior that hasn't gotten into in trouble one year prior to being nominated. Which meant, that if you got into any trouble involving drugs or alcohol throughout your high school years, you automatically couldn't be on court. I was safe, I'd never gotten in trouble that involved drugs or alcohol and the last time that I had gotten in any trouble at all was three years ago when I was a freshmen. But the coolest thing of all is that all the students in the entire school nominate you. There would be six girls and six boys for the entire school to choose to be their Winterfest King and Winterfest Queen, and I was one of them.

The way that the student counsel committee goes about making everyone aware of who's going to be on court is by acting out skits in order to get the crowd to try and guess who they're imitating. My skit was probably the eighth skit to be preformed. As I sat watching my fellow nominees skits, I just so happened to glance across to the freshmen section and who did I see standing there, my mom. Amy and Simone both seen my mom as well, they then told me that they had known that entire weekend that I was going to be on court, and so did my parents. Amy and Simone proceed to tell me that they were the ones that gave the student counsel skit ideas for me. They wouldn't tell me what they'd told the committee but I'd soon find out.

It was now time for my skits, and they consisted of Amy and I having "Hi contests", this is when we would walk around school together and see who could get the most people to say hi to them, and I'd always win. In high school I was very much into make up and I always wore fake diamond rhinestones by the corner of my eyes. So, one of my skits consist of a girl pretending to be me in front of a mirror doing her make up. She would then turn around with big silver star stickers by the corner of her eyes to imitate my diamonds rhinestones.

But the funniest skit of all was the skit that involved a swimming pool. I'd never learned how to swim so one day during the summer I decided to go out and buy a kiddy swimming pool. But I didn't stop there; I then filled it up with water and invited Amy, Simone, Jamie, and Monica over to go swimming with me in my new pool. Once they all arrived at my house they'd realize that it was a kiddy pool and then I'd tell them that we'd have to take turns swimming. We all got a kick out of it, but I couldn't believe that they told that story to the student counsel committee.

Then Mr. Gavin, the teacher who was in charge of this event announced, "your 2003 Winterfest court nominee is Timesha Mullins"! And the crowd went crazy. It was one of the most wonderful but yet unexplainable moments in my life. I stood up from the bleachers and proceeded to make my way onto the court. As I walked down from the bleachers slowly trying not to fall, two students ran around the court with signs in there hands, one said "Timesha" in big colorful letters and the other one said "Mullins" in big colorful letters as well. Once I reached the bottom of the bleachers I was greeted by a gentlemen who then presented me with an orange rose, which is our school color and we walked arm in arm down the court over to my seat, which was in front of twelve hundred students.

It was about a two-hour process to get all of the twelve nominees onto the court. Our pep rally was now over, we received a round of applause from our fellow classmates, and school was now back in session. All twelve nominees were informed that we didn't have to go to class because we were excused for the morning to go out for breakfast and do whatever else we wanted to do. I then went over and gave my mom a hug and talked to her briefly, because she had to get back to work and plus us twelve nominees were going out to breakfast.

We all decided as a group that were we going to eat breakfast at a local 24-hour opened restaurant known as Perkins. After breakfast, all twelve of us headed back to school. It was the beginning of February and the roads were extremely icy that day. As I proceeded to drive back from Perkins I decided to take the lake road back to school. The lake road is located by the big and small lakes, which are also located directly behind my high school. I remember it as if it was yesterday, I was driving back from Perkins in my 1993 Maroon Chevy Corsica, singing along to Ashanti "Happy", when all of a sudden my car started sliding all over the road.

The roads were very slippery and my car was now sliding all over and I was quickly approaching a sharp turn. And that's when it happened. I ran into a parked City van, and my car came to a complete stop. I sat there in disbelief that I had just gotten into a car accident. I remember felling extremely sad because I had been having a great day and now it was ruined. I had just gotten on court, and now I had to make a phone call and tell my parents that I had crashed into a parked City van.

I had just seen my mom at school a few hours earlier when I had gotten onto Winterfest court, so I didn't want to bother her because she had already taken time off from work that day. So, I called my dad, he worked the eleven at night until seven in the morning shift and it was early in the afternoon so I knew that he'd be at home sleeping. My dad is a heavy sleeper and I knew that he might not even hear the phone ring. But I called anyway and to my surprise he answered.

The first words out of his mouth were "Congratulations Timesha for getting on Winterfest court". I quickly replied, "thanks, but we have a big problem, I just got in a car accident"! But he didn't believe me because I joke around all the time. He then asked me if I was serious, was I okay, what had happened, and then told me to sit tight that he was on his way and that he would sending a police officer out to the site as well. And that's exactly what I did, sat tight until my dad arrived.

This was my first car accident but it wouldn't me my last. To this day I've been in about ten accidents. Most of them were small accident that weren't even my fault. These accidents would include anything from me running into a parked van, me running over a cat, me being side swiped by another car, me being rear ended by another car, me being hit by a taxi cab, but my last as well as the worst accident of all was only months away. It's kind of funny, because any kind of trouble I got into my dad would always be the first person to come to check on me and see if I was okay, and each time he'd always bet the police officer on duty.

It was now February 7, 2003 and once again I was sitting in the middle of the twelve hundred students that attended my school. It was a matter of seconds before everyone would know who our 2003 Winterfest king and queen were. I remember that right before the pep rally took place that the twelve of us all got together and ate lunch at one of the fellow nominees house. We all ate lunch, watched a movie, and then wished each other good luck as we went our separate ways to prepare for the pep rally.

It's kind of funny, because of course we all wanted to win, but at the same time we knew that only two of us could win. So, for that one week it was like we were a family, we spent a lot of time together and never once did we have an argument. I remember that many of the nominees were going around school sparking up conversations with people that they normally wouldn't even said "hi" to. But not Timesha, I had always been nice to everyone, and I figured whatever happened was meant to be. Plus, I wasn't going to go out of my way by pretending to be someone that I wasn't just to snag an extra vote.

It was now time for the king and queen to be crowned. We all noticed that when we walked onto the court that there were twelve seats as well as twelve plastic bowling pins that sat in front of each seat. The twelve of us split up into six separate groups, one guy with one girl, and then walked over to our assigned seats. In order to find out who the Winterfest king and queen were, we were each giving a plastic ball and told to roll the ball towards the pin in front of us on the count of three. Once the pins were knocked over the king and queen would have a red X on the bottom of their pins.

On the count of three we all rolled our balls and balls as well as pins went flying everywhere. We each held up our pins so that everyone could see them. My pin had a red X on the bottom of it and so did Chris's. The crowd went crazy as Mr. Gavin announced "your 2003 Winterfest king and queen are Chris Smith and Timesha Mullins. Chris and I stood in the middle of the court as we got our pictures taken for the Daily News and our school year book. We had hundred of people coming up to us congratulating us and telling us that they voted for us.

Both of my parents were there as well as my ten month old little brother Peter. My family as well as my friends rushed over to congratulate me. Of course my dad had been video taping the whole thing, and now my mom had to get pictures of me and my king as well as me and my friends. Both of my parents were extremely proud of me. But my mom by far, was more excited then I could have ever been. I remember that afterwards a lot of people came up and told me that I didn't look happy once I found out that I had won. I was extremely happy to be crowned as the Winterfest queen, but I think that I was more in shock than anything. I knew going into the whole thing that I had a pretty good chance of winning. And once I won, it took me awhile to grasp the fact that I had indeed won.

My senior year in high school, as well as the best year of my life, was quickly coming to an end. But not without me being recognized a little more. In March I was invited to attend a Community Service seminar in St.Paul, MN. I attended this seminar with two teachers from my school and three other students. At this seminar I gave two ten minute speeches to teachers from different schools in Minnesota explaining the reasoning behind the community service class as well as why they should have this class as an option at their schools. I explained to them how students visiting local elementary schools as well as nursing homes could truly have a great impact on the individual as well as the community. I was presented a Community Service award at the City Hall for doing this as well.

In May of 2003, I was invited to be on television. A local station in town was doing a segment titled "Making the Grade". This was a half an hour special that dealt with the class of 2003. I was one of the six students chosen from over two hundred and forty to be a part of this broadcast. It was a great experience, I very much enjoyed the idea that I was going to be on television, but even more I liked the idea that someone had chosen me to do so. I thought the whole idea behind the "Making the Grade" broadcast was great. Because whether people realize it or not graduating from high school is a great accomplishment and to have someone give you an half an hour of air time to express what your high school years were like, really meant a lot.

On May 21, 2003 my family and I were invited to attend Student Reconization night at my high school. This was an event that was hosted yearly for the graduating seniors. It's kind of funny, because the week before I had seen Mr. Kruse and he had asked me if I was going and I told him that I hadn't been invited. He then turned and smiled at me and said "but who's to say that you won't". The next day my family and I received an invitation in the mail. I'm usually pretty good at reading between the lines and figuring out what's going on. But on this night I was completely clueless.

I remember sitting in my chair reading the schedule of events for that night. I sat next to a girl by the name of Stacy. Stacy is a girl that I met my junior year in high school and although we didn't hang out outside of school, we were still close friends. We both noticed that there were hundreds of names with writing behind them explaining what scholarships and awards they were receiving. But then once we came across our names, there was nothing was behind either one, this had both of us extremely puzzled because we couldn't understand why we were there. But both of us would soon find out.

Mr. Kruse then stood up and began to talk about how proud he was of all of the graduating seniors and that we've come a long way. He also talked about how many students today are totally different people than they were the first day that the entered high school. It was at this time that Stacy and I both were presented with a "Winhawk Growth Award". The Winhawk Growth Award is giving to two of the graduating seniors who the school board feels have changed a great deal from the first day they walked into high school until the last day they walked out.

Out of all the awards that I have received in my entire life, I would have to say that this was the one that I was most proud of. I was most proud of this award because I had done the unexpected. I entered high school as a scared and confused fourteen-year-old girl whose mother had just been sent to prison and was now being put into a foster home as well as being separated from her brothers. But I was exiting high school as a very confident as well as determined eighteen-year-old that wasn't going to let anyone or anything get in the way of her fulfilling her dreams.

To me, the Winhawk Growth Award was an award that showcased how one can easily turn something negative into something positive with the help of a support team. My support team from September 1999 through May 2003 consisted of only four people: Kelly (my mom), Bryan (my dad), Mr. Kruse (my guardian angel), and Yolanda (my grandmother). These were the four people that were always there for me no matter what. I knew I could count on them for anything, because they'd always be there to help me out in my time of need.

Chapter 12
Triumph to Tragedy

I graduated from Winona Senior High School on June 6, 2003. This was truly a special day. I couldn't believe that I had actually made it through high school, and was now graduating. My mom's parents, Harry and Sally had come into town to celebrate me graduating and so did Grandma Yolanda. I had also invited Grandpa Barry and his wife Beth as well, but Beth called me the week before and told me that they wouldn't be able to make it because my grandfather was sick in the hospital (his lungs had collapsed). But I was still happy, because it was five o'clock in the evening and I would be graduating in just two hours.

My family and I, along with Kelly's parents, and Grandma Yolanda all went out to dinner at a Chinese restaurant. It was my special day and I got to pick a place for us to eat. My first choice was McDonald's because I love their french fries, but that didn't fly over to well with the parents. So, of course my next choice would have to be an all you can eat Chinese buffet. During dinner my mom was extremely excited because she had brought one of my gifts to dinner and wanted me too open it right away. It was a small box and I knew it was jewelry, so I opened it in a hurry. It was a beautiful white gold diamond necklace with a matching white gold diamond ring. She asked me if I liked it and I told her that I loved it. I wore the necklace to my graduation that night; the ring was too big so we had to get it sized.

After dinner, my parents dropped me off at the high school so I could get my graduation pictures taken, and then I would ride on the bus over to the college university, which is where the graduation ceremony was to be held. I remember that as I was running to catch my bus I heard someone yell "Me-Me". Me-Me was a nickname that I had when I was younger, as well as the name that my younger brother Jacob used to call me. At the age of eighteen, no one referred to me as Me-Me except Egg and my relatives back in Illinois. I then turned around and there stood Egg.

I told her that I had no time to stop and talk to her. She then told me that she just wanted to congratulate me and give me a hug. I agreed, she gave me a hug and then said, "Look at my baby girl; I'm so proud of you". I then told her that I had to go and ran to catch up with my friends. I must admit that seeing Egg before my I graduated kind of put me in a bad mood. I knew that she was going to be there but I was hoping that I wouldn't have to see or talk to her until afterwards.

The one thing that upset me the most was her saying "look at my baby girl; I'm so proud of you". Proud of me indeed she may have been, but the one thing that she failed to realize is that she had absolutely nothing at all to do with the person that I had become. And most of, she didn't even know me anymore. She still looked and talked to me as if I was fourteen-years-old, and that's what pissed me off the most, she didn't want to accept the fact that I was now an adult.

I decided that this was my special day and that I wasn't going to let anything or anyone ruin it, including Egg. I remembered feeling overwhelmed as well as extremely hot as I walked into the auditorium of the college. Although everyone was told not too cheer, families still cheered the names of their children, including my family. I remember looking up into the bleachers and seeing hundreds of people. My parents and grandparents got front row seats due to the fact that Grandma Yolanda is disabled (she has to walk with a cane from the stroke she suffered from back in 1996). I then glanced up and saw my brothers Mitchell and Jacob sitting with their parents Suzanne and Robert, and I even saw Egg sitting with her friend Vera. The graduation ceremony lasted a little over two hours, and once it was done everyone went home or back to their hotel rooms to get plenty of rest because the next day was Timesha's Graduation Party.

I would honestly have to say that my graduation party had a great turn out, regardless of the fact that seventy-five percent on the people that I graduated with were having their parties on the exact day. My party was on June 7th from one in the afternoon until four. I must admit that the first hour went by very slow and I remember thinking that no one was going to attend my party. But my mom made me feel a lot better by telling me that "don't worry honey, people will show up in due time. Plus no one likes to be the first person to arrive at a party".

She was right as usual, by the time two o'clock rolled around people started coming non-stop. All of which included my friends both old and new, family, co-workers, and even a few teachers from my high school attended my party. Mr. Kruse attended my party, as well as my high school principal. The school secretary came out to congratulate me, as did my foods teacher, and my math teacher. But the guest that I was most excited to see was Mrs. Hanson.

Mrs. Hanson was my ninth grade English in 1999 and she retired in 2000. Even though she didn't teach at my school anymore we still kept in contact with each other. Anytime that I was in the newspaper she would write me a little sweet letter along with a copy of the article and mail it to my house. I would then send her a thank you card in return. This is the relationship that we had my entire senior year in high school, so once she showed up at my graduation party I was extremely surprised as well as shocked. I hadn't seen Mrs. Hanson in almost three years and for her and her husband to attend my graduation party just meant the world to me.

I very much so enjoyed the graduation party that my parents threw for me, as did everyone that attended. The only part about the party that I didn't like, as did many other people that attended, is the fact that Egg was there. I wouldn't have been a big deal if Egg had come to my party to congratulate me, eat some food, and then left. But no, Egg had to come to my party that my parents, not her threw for me, broadcasting to everyone that I was her daughter and how proud of me she was. As well as feeling my brothers' heads with a bunch of bullshit about how they didn't belong with Suzanne and Richard, and that it was just a matter of time before the four of us would be together again.

The sad thing was that my brothers and I hadn't lived with Egg in over fours, in which these four years my brothers had been adopted, and I was now an adult. So needless to say, there was no way in hell that we would have ever considered living with her again. Egg didn't personally talk to me about any of her plans of us being together. However, she did discuss them with my brothers. According to my brothers, Egg talked about us being together again, and I believed them, as did everyone else. There's no way in hell that anyone would believe Egg over Mitchell and Jacob, it just wouldn't happen.

My graduation party would end with me trying to help my parents clean up and them telling me that they didn't need my help. I would then venture my way over to my Simone's house to attend her graduation party, but not before receiving a phone call from Nichole. During this phone conversation we talked about a wild hotel party that we both attended back in April. I was fully aware that Nichole hadn't gotten her period in a while. It was during this conversation that Nichole told me that she had taken a pregnancy test after she let my party, and I came back positive, which met that she was pregnant. Nichole told me that she was pregnant and that she wanted me to be the Godmother.

The beginning of June was a happy time for my family and I. But, tragedy would soon strike as the middle of June quickly approached us. This would happen on June 28, 2003 when Bryan's mother Tracy and her boyfriend Greg were driving back from the casino. The casino is located in Red Wing, MN, which is about a sixty-minute drive from the town we live in. Tracy and Greg took turns driving to Red Wing almost every weekend. On this particular day Greg decided that he would drive Tracy's car from the casino back home.

From what I've been told, they were driving down Highway 61 at about sixty miles an hour and everything seemed to be going well. Then all of a sudden, Greg began to have a seizure. I'm sure Tracy went into an immediate panic, but at the same time she still some how managed to gain control of the car and pull it over to the side of the highway. Tracy and I both had just received new cell phones from my parents in the Christmas of 2002, and that is how she was able to call 911 and direct help to the location of which they were located.

It was at this point that Tracy started performing CPR on Greg. This is what she would spend the next half an hour doing until the paramedics arrived. Once emergency help arrived, it was too late. Greg's heart had stopped beating. However, the paramedics were able to revive him, and he was then transported to one of the best hospitals in the world, the Mayo Clinic, which is located in Rochester, MN. Once they arrived to the hospital, Greg was immediately put on life support.

Greg would spend three days in the hospital fighting for his life. From what I've been told, it took the doctors about a day and a half to come to the conclusion that Greg was brain dead. It was at this point of time that both Greg's family s and Tracy's family came to stand by Greg's side as he fought a battle that we will all have fight someday. Greg's three sons were going through the most pain. As sad as it was, all three of them knew that their father's life was in their hands.

June 30, 2003 was the day that I was supposed to drive to Rochester to visit Greg in the hospital. I remember that my mom called me from the hospital and advised me not to come because things weren't looking too good. She also told me that Greg's three sons had decided that they could no longer bear to witness their father suffer as he had been for the past three days and that they had decided to pull the plug, by taking him off of life support. The afternoon of June 30, 2003, was the day that Greg left this earth and transitioned into heaven to live another life.

Although I had only known Greg for four years, his death still had a great impact on my life. Greg was the first person in my entire life that I had actually known who had died. I mean of course I had heard stories of family members that had passed away, but that didn't affect me in anyway, shape, or form, for the simple fact that I didn't know them. But I knew Greg and had known him for years. I remember looking at a photo that my dad had taken of me, Greg, and Tracy at my graduation party. The three of us looked happy in the picture and all three of us had no idea that in less than two weeks one of us would be gone.

Greg's funeral was held on July 2, 2003 and everyone came together to say their final good-byes. I remember feeling a great deal of sadness as I glanced at Greg's ex-wife, his sons, and his grandchildren. His ex-wife had just lost a man that she had loved for many years as well as the father of her children. His sons had just lost the man that they had referred to as "dad" their entire lives and two of them had to try and stay strong for their own children. And his infant grandchildren would be one grandparent short. They wouldn't have any memories of their own, but I'm sure they will hear great stories about their Grandpa Greg, as they grow older.

I then remember that I sat on the left hand side of Tracy and I remembered thinking to myself "this poor woman". I felt a great deal of pain for Tracy because it had seemed as if everything see loved was somehow taken away from her. Her husband Steve had been taken away from her by cancer, her son Peter had been killed in a house fire, and now, more than two decades later the man that she had loved dearly for many years had been taken away from her as well. I remember sitting next to her as we both cried.

It was even sadder to see Greg being put to rest. Greg had been in the military for many years and as he was put to rest gunshots were fired in his honor. I remember that everyone was crying as a couple of military men folded an American flag and handed it to Greg's three sons, they walked away in tears. As did everyone else who stood there and watched.

Chapter 13
Talk of the Town

It was now the middle of July, and this is when I would receive my final award before I headed off to college. I had been working at the grocery store for two and a half years and my hard work was finally about to be recognized. On this particular day that I was working I remember that I was checking a customer out at the cash register, as well as helping her bag her groceries. I noticed that the customer behind her was holding something in her arms that didn't look like groceries. She also had a big camera tied around her neck. I didn't think much of it and I continued with what I was doing.

Just as I got done bagging the customer groceries and putting them into her cart, I noticed that the owner of the grocery store was walking towards me with a smile on his face. It was also at this exact time that the office door which is located in front of the check out lanes, swung open and two mangers walked out. It was at that exact moment that the customer who was next in line with the camera tied around her neck turned to me and said "Timesha Mullins, I'm here to present you with a award from the Commerce for being the most hospitable person in the community"!

I was totally taken by surprise. My exact words were "Oh my God, are you serious"? And everyone laughed, including me. The lady then told me that she needed a picture of me with my award because I was going to be in the newspaper. I stood there with the award in my hand and smiled as a ton of people surrounded me including: the owner of the store, managers, co-workers, and even customers. Everyone was extremely proud of me and they all wanted to congratulate me. With all of the people that I was surrounded by I felt as if I were a famous actress or singer.

The most hospitable person in the community is an award that is giving out each month. This is done when members of the Commerce go around to various businesses in town to secretly watch how employees treat their customers. I guess a member must have come through my line at the grocery store in the month of July of 2003 and received outstanding service; otherwise I wouldn't have been given the award.

My parents were very pleased with me receiving this award, so of course they took me out for Chinese food. The owner of the grocery store was extremely pleased as well and he gave me a card with a fifty-dollar bill inside to show his appreciation. But the coolest thing of all was that my family and I were invited to an appreciation night that was held by members of the commerce. We would get to eat dinner, receive small gifts from a raffle, and I would be recognized for being "The most hospitable person in the community".

It was now the middle of July and things were going pretty well, but that would all change on July 22, 2003. The afternoon of July 22, 2003 was a sunny afternoon. I was hanging out over at my best friend Nichole's house. We had been sitting around all day long with nothing to do. So, when a girl by the name of Brittany called my cell phone and asked if I'd come and pick her up then give her a ride to her house, I said "Sure, it's not like I have anything else to do"!

I no longer had the Chevy Corsica due to an accident that I was in. I had been side swiped by another vehicle and on top of that I also needed a new transmission, so I decided that I should just buy another car. I loved my new car a lot. But even more so, I loved the fact that I had bought it myself with money that I had saved, just like I did with the Corsica. I was the only one out of all my friends that drove, that actually bought my own cars. Everyone was so amazed at how I was able to buy the Corsica for $1,700 and then turn around just seven months later and buy the Intrepid for $3,200. That's when I replied, "I worked my ass off each summer, and saved all my money". Of course it wasn't my idea to save the money it was my parents and they set up the account so that I so that I couldn't touch the money. By the time I was seventeen I had over $8,000 in my saving account. But that would all disappear within a year. Once I turned eighteen, and was now legally allowed to get my money out of my savings account, I spent it all on cars, clothes, shoes, weed, alcohol and food.

Both Nichole and I hopped into my two month old Purple 1996 Dodge Intrepid, opened the sunroof and off we went. Brittany told me that she was over at a friend's house that lived in the exact same low-income complex that my brothers and I had lived in just four years earlier with Egg. So, I knew exactly where she was. As Nichole and I turned into the complex, we noticed that there were a lot of little kids playing in a local park. We also noticed that Brittany was standing outside on the corner and joked around about her being in a hurry to go home. I pulled up by Brittany and honked my horn just to be funny, and Brittany hopped into my car. Nichole and I then asked Brittany if she wanted to watch a movie with us over at Nichole's house and she said yes, and I proceeded to drive off back to Nichole's house.

The plan was for the three of us to head back over to Nichole's house to eat some food and watch a movie. But this would all change within a matter of seconds. I switched my car from "park" to "drive" and slowly pulled away from the curb. I hadn't even driven a half of block, and could've been going more than thirteen miles per hour. And that's when it happened. A four-year-old little girl ran out into the street from behind a parked van, and I hit her.

I slammed on the brakes so hard that Brittany, who wasn't wearing her seat belt, flew out of her seat into the front between Nichole and I. I also hit the brakes so hard that both the driver and passenger visors flew down as well as open. It was at this point that all three of us started screaming that we didn't see the little girl and that she came out of no where. I put my car in park, unbuckled my seat belt, then jumped out of my car and hurried to the front of my car where I knew the little girl was.

I will never forget that the first words out of my mouth were "Oh my God, I just hit a little girl with my car! I'm going to jail"! I then kneeled down by the little girl and asked her if she was okay, and she told me she was fine and that she just wanted to go home! The little girl then attempted to get up off the ground. But she couldn't get off the ground because she couldn't move her right leg. It was unlike anything that I had ever seen in my entire life. She was lying on the ground in front of my car with her right thigh and knee turned inward touching her left thigh and knee, while the right part of her leg and her right foot was facing upward.

It was at this point that I immediately used my cell phone to call for emergency help. I also ordered Nichole and Brittany to talk to the little girl and try to keep her calm but not to let her try and get up off the ground. As I talked on the phone to the 911 dispatcher and told her what had happen and that I needed an ambulance, the little girl overheard me and started screaming, that she was ok and that she didn't want to go to the doctor, because she was scared of the doctor. It was also at this point that I noticed that a group of maybe six or seven little kids from the local park had started to gather around.

Once I was done talking to the 911 dispatcher and I knew that help was on the way, I started asking all the little kids around me if they knew who the little girl was, where her parents were, or even if they knew where she lived. The kids knew nothing; they didn't even remember her name. All they could tell me was that they had been playing at the park with her early and that she took off running out into the streets without looking both ways. This information really didn't help me out at all.

It was at this point that a woman walked up to me and told me that she knew who the little girl was and that she lived "over there". The direction that the woman pointed in was the opposite direction in which the little girl was headed. The women then ordered a younger child that was standing near by to go and get the little girls parents. It was at this point that many more people had started to gather around. My friends and I stood in complete silence.

I stood in front of my parked car in the middle of the street with strangers surrounding and pointing at me. I looked at the little girl who was trying so hard to get up off the ground and to go home and felt nothing but sorrow and guilt. It was at that exact moment that I heard police, ambulance, and fire trucks sirens in the background. Just as the emergency vehicles turned the corner the little girls parents came running from around the opposite direction in which their daughter had been running in earlier.

The little girl's parents made it over within seconds of the paramedics rushing out of their ambulance with their equipment. The little girl's parents kneeled down by her and once they saw the condition she was in, they immediately began to cry. It was at this point that the little girl who had been trying so hard to make her way home, for the first time throughout the whole ordeal, began to cry as well. I stood off to the side in complete disbelief. I couldn't believe that any of this was actually happening.

My friends and I stood off to the side and I noticed reporters from the Daily News were on the scene snapping pictures and my heart dropped. I sincerely hoped that this doesn't come off as me sounding conceded but, I was known very well in town for doing good things and the last thing that I wanted was to be looked down on because of an accident. Because that's exactly what it was, an accident. It wasn't my fault nor was it the little girl's fault. We were both just in the wrong place at the wrong time.

It was at this point that a police officer came over and took a statement from me, Nichole, Brittany, and the little kids from the park that had witnessed the accident. Once everyone was done given their statements the police officer told me that I should call home and let my parents know what had happened. And once again my heart dropped. I was fully aware that this was one of the worst phone calls that my parents could have ever received from me. I mean sure I'd been in numerous car accidents, but none of which had ever involved anyone being hospitalized.

I picked up my phone and dialed my home phone number. My mom answered the phone and to my surprise, the phone call wasn't nearly as bad as I expected. My mom answered the phone on the first ring and told me to make it quick because she was on the other line taking to her friend Dana. My mom and Dana had been co-workers as well as friends for years. Dana was also the mother of my friend and soon to be roommate Simone. I agreed to make it quick and told her that I had been in an accident and hit a little girl with my car. And she didn't believe me. She then told me to stop joking around and that she would call me right back because she was just about to get off the phone with Dana. And we both hung up the phone.

It was within a matter of seconds from us hanging up the phone with each other, that my phone rang. It was my mom. She was talking extremely fast and asking me if I had really hit a little girl with my car because Dana had just heard something come across her police scanner about a four-year-old girl getting hit by a car. I told her that it was me that what they were talking about and that it was true. I had indeed hit a little girl with my car. My mom then immediately began to apologize to me, she told me that she was sorry for not believing me because I joke around all the time and then she began asking me if I was okay and if the little girl was seriously injured. I told her that it was all over with now and that the little girl was being taken to the hospital.

So, the little girl in her parents took off to the hospital in an ambulance and my friends and I were free to leave. I remember thinking 'What, I'm not going to jail'? I also remember asking the police officer if he needed to take pictures of the scene or use a tape measurer to measure the distance from my car to when the little girl was. But he assured me that they didn't do anything like that, it was only in the movies that they do stuff like that. I remember that I had never been so scared in my entire life, but everyone of the scene was extremely nice to me. And after the ambulance drove away with the little girl and her parents inside I was free to go as well.

I drove away feeling like I was a disgrace to society. I couldn't bare to go home; although my mom was very sympathetic about the whole thing I just couldn't do it. I just couldn't take my mind off what had just happened. Nichole, Brittany, and I all decided that none of us were in the mood to watch a movie anymore. Instead we drove down by the big lake and sat outside on a near by park bench for at least two hours. We were all in shock; none of us could grasp what had actually happen. We spoke to each other periodically, but for the most part we just sat in silence and watched the geese swim in the water.

The next day was one of the most difficult days in my life. I woke up thinking that it had all been a dream. But it was true; my dad's sister Connie came over early that morning and told my family and I that a local radio station had talked about the accident earlier that morning. I then decided to call the hospital the day after the accident to see how the little girl was doing, but they couldn't and wouldn't tell me anything, unlike in the movies. It's kind of funny how things in real life are nothing like they are in the movies. I also sent the little girl a beautiful bouquet of flowers, a teddy bear and a "Get well soon" card. I had no clue as to how this little girl was doing. I would later learn, while switching car insurance companies, that the little girl had sustained a dislocated thigh from the accident.

After I went to the local flower shop and bought the little girl a bouquet of flowers, a teddy bear, and a "Get well soon" card, I decided to stop by a gas station to read what the Daily News had to say about this whole situation. But to my surprise, it wasn't in the paper. I can honestly say that for two weeks straight I woke up bright and early and drove down to the gas station and bought a paper. I bought as well as read the Daily News for two weeks straight, but there was never an article nor and picture about the accident.

I was puzzled I had seen the Daily News crew on site taking pictures so I just couldn't understand why it wasn't in the paper. I lived in a town of about 35,000 people and everything goes in the Daily News anything from a DWI, minor consumption, or even a traffic ticket. I read many articles in the paper for those two weeks, but none of them involved "Timesha Mullins". And this is what pissed a lot of people off the most.

I would be the talk of the low income complex from July 22, 2003, the day of the accident until August 21, 2003, the day that both Simone and I moved to Rochester, MN to attend college. There was talk about the little girls parents suing me for hitting their daughther. Many people changed the story around and were now saying that I was high and drunk when I hit the little girl and that I drug her twenty feet before stopping. When in reality I was around four in the afternoon, I was completely sober, and if I could turn back the hands of time the accident wouldn't have took place at all. But the accident wasn't nearly as bad as everyone was hyping it up to be. I merely bumped the little girl with the front of my car. It wasn't like I had actually driven over her with all four of my tires.

So, now there's talk about me getting sued, and that I was high and drunk when I hit the little girl, and I knew that it was just a matter of time before people would start to say "The reason why Timesha didn't get into any trouble is because her dad works for the police department"! People just couldn't understand why the accident wasn't in the paper, why I didn't get arrested, or why the police officers didn't issue me a reckless driving ticket. Although it's very true that I didn't get into any trouble at all, it had absolutely nothing to do with my dad working for the police department.

I must admit that I was surprised of the outcome myself. I didn't go to jail, the accident wasn't in the newspaper, I wasn't issued a reckless driving ticket, my insurance didn't go up, and in the end the little girls parents didn't even try to sue me. And to this day I still believe all of this to be true for three reasons: 1) I placed the 911 call, 2) the little girls parents weren't around when the accident occurred, and the most important reason of all, 3) the little kids that witnessed the accident while playing at the near by park.

Chapter 14
Friend or Foe

August 21, 2003 was the day that Simone and I moved to Rochester, MN to attend college. We had made prior arrangements to live in the four bedroom dorms that were located directly behind RCTC (Rochester Community Technical College). We would also be rooming with two sisters by the names of Denise and Eliza. I was extremely excited to be moving to Rochester because in my eyes, it was like I was a brand new person. No one would know who I was, where I was from, where I had been or where I was going. It was my chance to reinvent myself. And I was excited.

The morning of August 21, 2003 was a foggy morning, but after driving for an hour to Rochester it was now sunny. It was a very exciting day for both Simone and I. We were both eighteen years old and in a matter of hours we would be free to do as we pleased. Now I don't know about Simone's parents, but I do know that even though I was moving an hour away, that my parents we still sad to see me go. I remember just moments before my parents and I headed to Rochester that I walked past the bathroom and saw my mom standing in front of the bathroom sink, and through the reflection of the mirror, I could see that she was crying.

I walked into the bathroom and ran my fingers through her hair. That's the one way that I know how to comfort her when she's sad. There was no need for me to ask her why she was crying because I already knew. I told her not to worry that I was only moving an hour away and that I would come home every weekend. She then stopped crying, put her sunglasses on, and then we were off to Rochester. My parents and my little brother Peter, Simone's parents, and Simone's older brother Ryan and his girlfriend Vanessa all drove ahead of us in three separate vehicles, while Simone and I both trailed behind them in separate vehicles as well.

We arrived in Rochester in the early afternoon and unloaded all of our belongings. Simone and I immediately began setting up our bedrooms. Both of our dads began hooking up our cable to the television and hooking up the computer. While our moms, Ryan, and Vanessa all sat on the couch talking to each other as well as watching Peter entertained them. After Simone and I were done setting up our rooms, we all decided to go and grab a quick bit to eat. Simone and I both decided that we wanted to eat a Wendy's, so that's where we ate. After we were done eating my dad decided that I needed a fan for my bedroom, so both of our dads along with, Ryan, Vanessa, and Peter went to go and buy me a fan as well as some other things that I needed from a near by store, while Simone and I went grocery shopping with our moms.

It was now more than two hours later and everyone was back at our apartment. My mom and Dana had spent nearly three hundred dollars on food for the both of us. My dad had also gone out and bought me the most expensive fans that he could find and it even came with a remote control. After Simone and I were done putting our groceries away, we hugged and kissed our parent's good-bye as they headed back home. As we watched their cars drive away, we both felt a sense of freedom. Simone then headed back to her room and told me to stay in the living room because she had a surprise for me. Within a matter on seconds, Simone appeared before with pint of Bacardi Limon.

Simone and I then began to get drunk and then we decided that were we bored. We both knew that three boys of whom we had graduated with lived near by, so we called them up and told them that we wanted to hang out. We told them that we didn't want to drive because we had been drinking plus we didn't know where they lived, so one of the guys named Todd said that he would come and pick us up. The plan was for us to go over to their house and party for a while. We couldn't stay out all night because we had freshmen orientation the following morning. But that wasn't what happened.

I really was more of a pothead than a drinker in high school. But now that I was in college, that was all about to change. My first night in Rochester was the drunkest that I had ever gotten in my entire life. I had already been drinking earlier with Simone and now I was standing in the middle of Todd's living room taking Vodka shots. It was the first time that I had ever drinking Vodka before, and once I tried it, I took an immediate liking to it. I liked it so much that I took twelve shots within a half an hour and passed out.

I don't exactly remember how or when I made it back home that night. But I do know that I woke up the following morning in my bed. I also woke up with one of the worst headaches in my entire life, as well as puking into a trashcan that was already filled with vomit from the night before. Needless to say neither Simone nor I made it to freshmen orientation that day. This would be the first of many drunken nights to come for both Simone and I. But in due time we wouldn't be spending them together.

It was now the beginning of October and Simone and I were once again packing or belongings and preparing to move. Simone and I thought that we got along great with Denise and Eliza. I mean sure Simone and I partied a lot but we'd always ask them before hand if it would be alright for us to have company over, and they'd always say that it was fine. But secretly both Denise and Eliza along with their parents had a meeting with the manager of the dorms and complained about us parting too much. One of the rules in the dorms is that your apartment can only receive three warnings and then you'll be evicted, but still have to pay your rent until the end of the school year.

By the time October rolled around, Simone and I already had two. One was for having a party the first weekend before school even started and getting the police called to our apartment, and the other was for having our upstairs and downstairs neighbor's complaint about playing our music too loud. The manger of Evanston Heights gave us the choice of either relocating or being evicted, so needless to say, we choice to relocate. But we weren't the only ones having problems with our roommates.

A friend of ours by the name of Kimberly who we had also gone to high school with us was also having roommate problems. So, the manager of the dorms decided to give us our very own apartment. I was excited; me, Simone, Kimberly, and a girl by the name of Amber Diekmann were going to be roommates. Amber was the only previous roommate that had gotten along with, and she decided to move in with us. Now Kimberly loved to party like Simone and I but when it came to Amber that was a different story. She didn't party at all, but instead she studied.

Lindsay Dick and Alexa House were the names of Kimberly and Amber's old roommates. Neither Simone, Amber, nor I had any problems with these girls at all. Simone and I both had partied with them on many occasions. And as for the reasoning behind Amber moving out of their apartment building was simply because she lived in apartment 840, which known very well as the party building. Amber knew that apartment 842; the building that we were moving into wasn't as noisy and was told by Kimberly that Simone and I were quiet. So Amber was under the impression that Simone and I didn't party. This led Amber to believe that she would be moving into a noise free environment. This meant that she could for once study in peace. Amber would soon find this to be very untrue.

Now Kimberly's reason for moving out of the apartment with Lindsay and Alexa was totally different. I must admit that it did take me awhile to realize it. But the only reason why Kimberly moved out of her old apartment was simply because she was jealous of Alexa. This was made very clear do to the fact that once she and Amber moved in with Simone and I, she was still very much obsessed with talking about Alexa. She would always complaint about how she didn't like Alexa because she was too pretty, too skinny, too stuck up, and too rich. Minus the fact that Kimberly bitched about Alexa all the time, and the fact that Amber stayed in her room all the time. They were both great roommates, but that was all about to change.

Once Kimberly and Amber moved into a new apartment with Simone and I that meant that Lindsay and Alexa had to get two new roommates.

Lindsay and Alexa were now living with a Black and White Lesbian couple by the names of Gerry and Dawn. Both Gerry and Dawn were known all throughout the dorms as the "Interracial Lesbian couple that shared a bedroom". But they were also very much liked by everyone. So Lindsay and Alexa had no problem with them moving into their apartment.

By the time January of 2004 it was the second semester of school and Simone and I had drifted apart and she was now best friends with Gerry and Dawn. Kimberly had dropped out of school and was on the verge of being kicked out of the dorms because she hadn't paid her rent since August. Amber and I were now best friends. Although Amber rarely left her room, I'd always go into her room just to hang out, and we'd talk for hours. I remember one time that I even fell asleep on her bedroom floor.

My new best friends were Amber, Lindsay, and Alexa. It was also at this time that I was introduced to two girls by the names of Belle Patters who went by the name of and Sarah Sarkekey (Dick). Belle and Sarah were roommates that had been friends with Lindsay and Alexa since school had started. These were the five girls that I would spend the most time with. We'd party, go out to dinner, go shopping, watch movies, and occasionally we all do homework together. While Simone and I barley spoke to each other.

It's kind of funny because back in December 2003, Simone, Amber, and I had gone to management to complaint as well as try to get Kimberly kicked out of our apartment. All three of us told the manager that Kimberly never cleaning up after herself, was no longer helping us pay for utilities, and that she was even allowing her boyfriend to live in our apartment. All three of us agreed that we wanted Kimberly out of our apartment. The manager told us that she would see what she could do.

It was at this point that I took it upon myself to tell Kimberly that I had personally gone and told management that I no longer wanted to live with her. The reason behind me doing this was simple, I knew what I had done and I didn't want it to seem like I was talking about Kimberly behind her back, because that's not something that I'd do. So I told her to her face, "I'd rather tell you first before you hear it from management…" It was at this point that Kimberly locked herself in her room and only came out to eat, use the bathroom, and go to work. This would continue for well over a month.

But it was now January 2004 and Simone, Gerry, and Dawn had secretly arranged a meeting with the manager of the dorms. Simone had told management that she no longer wanted to live with me, Amber, or Kimberly, and that she would rather live with Gerry and Dawn. Gerry and Dawn had also told management that they no longer wanted to live with Lindsay and Alexa. I can't even imagine what else they told management about the four of us that day. But whatever they said must have been good because in the end, the manager of the dorms sided with them. It was at that point that management agreed with Simone and decided that Amber and I had to move to another apartment.

I'll never forget that it was around five in the afternoon on a Tuesday. Amber and I had just gotten back from Target and just as we approached the front door of apartment 842, the building that we lived in, we saw the manager of the dorms through the glass door walking down the stairs. Just as I was about to stick my key in the hole to open the door, she opened it and told Amber and I both "Both of you girls need to pack your stuff and be cleared out of this apartment by the end of the night"! And we both stood there with our mouths open in shock.

I remember calling my mom on the phone and telling her what had happened and how I felt so betrayed by Simone. Simone was supposed to have been my friend. I mean of course we were having problems but at least I had the decency to approach Simone and tell her how I felt. But Simone on the other hand couldn't do the same for me? Simone and I had known each other for years, so I was fully aware of the fact that she talked bad about many people behind their backs. But I thought she'd be better than that when it came to me, but I was wrong. I must admit that I was extremely hurt by the fact that Simone didn't come and talk to me first before the decision for Amber and I to move out was made. But I was even more hurt by the fact that she had thrown our friendship away for two girls that she had only known for two months.

I guess that it's no surprise that Amber and I moved into apartment 832 with Lindsay and Alexa and that Gerry and Dawn moved into our old apartment with Simone and Kimberly. It was also at this point that

Simone and Kimberly became friends all over again. And I'm willing to bet that to this day, Simone has never told Kimberly that she came right along with Amber and I and had tried to get Kimberly evicted. Instead I'm sure they both laughed about how big of a bitch I was and that they were glad that I was gone. I mean if people want to view me as being a bitch because I don't bite my tongue for anyone as well as the simple fact that I'm openly honest about the way I feel about someone, then fine, I guess I am a bitch.

Chapter 15

Good-Bye for Now

By the time March rolled around I was now nineteen years old. Also with all the drama now behind me now my living situation was going great. Why? Because I lived with three girls who weren't afraid to tell me if I was doing something that they didn't like. The same couldn't be said for Simone. She was now living in a four-bedroom apartment all by herself. Why? Because Management had decided that it was spring, the weather was nice, and now she could legally kick everyone out that hadn't been paying their rent.

This meant that Kimberly, along with Gerry and Dawn had to pack up their belongings and move elsewhere. I never really understood why Simone chose to live with three people who she knew hadn't paid their rent since August 2003. I'm sure that it was at this point Simone had realized that she had lost the only real friend she had, which was me. Simone and I would eventually start talking to each other again, but things would never be the same as they had been before.

My living situation was going extremely well, but school wise I was in trouble. I had breezed right through first semester and now as the end of second semester was quickly approaching I was pretty much failing all of my classes. It was at this point that I realized that I had a major problem. I drank too much. Vodka was my drink of choice, my new best friend, as well as the one thing that I devoted majority of my time too. I can honestly say that I drank five out of the seven days a week. It was also around this time that I began to notice another problem, and that problem was called sex. I'd have say the only reason behind me drinking was just so that I could have sex, and not feel bad about it afterwards. Because after all, I was only doing it when I was drunk.

I can very clearly see myself hanging out at a party, drinking, and just having a great time. But at the same time I'm thinking to myself "That guy's pretty cute, but that other guy is even cuter. I wonder which one of them I can get to come home with me tonight"? I realized that I had a problem then and I'm one hundred percent sure that I still have that exact same problem to this day. I have this need to always be wanted in a sexual way when it comes to men! I would have to say that nine out of ten times I'm the one that lures the guy to my house with one thing in mind, and that's sex. I know that there's a reason behind my promiscuous behavior, but at this point I am still unsure as to what it is.

Needless to say, my life wasn't going as good as it could've been, but I was the only one to blame for this. Aside from all of the bad that was happening, there was also some good. There was now a new addition to my family. April 19, 2004 was the day that mom and dad brought a beautiful little girl by the name of Nina into this world. It was at this point that I now had the little sister that I always wanted. It's kind of funny because Peter's birthday is April 5th, my dad's birthday is April 12th, my mom's birthday is April 21st, Nina was just born on April 19th, and then there Timesha's birthday which falls on March 4th. But needless to say, I'd always get the best gifts.

I will never forget that just by chance, April 19, 2004 was the day that I made my weekly visit back home to spend time with the family. I'd gotten into town around three thirty in the afternoon and my mom and I had plans to go and pick my dad out some fishing stuff for his birthday. My dad's birthday was the week before and I wasn't in town nor did I know what to get him. So, my mom decided that we would both go shopping together once I got into town, and she would then help me pick out a birthday gift for him.

As soon as I got into to my mom told me that we had to hurry up and go shopping and then come straight back home. She told me that she wasn't feeling well. She said that she was having some stomach pains. I told her that she didn't have to come shopping with me but she insisted on going anyway. But my mom's stomach pains weren't the reason for her wanting to hurry back home. My mom wanted to hurry back home because she was in the process of preparing a special dinner for me. She was making her famous smoked baked ham as well as here famous sour cream baked potato casserole dish, and I was excited I.

We left for the house around four in the evening and arrived back shortly after four thirty. Dinner was scheduled for six o'clock as it always had been. But little did we know that there would be no family dinner tonight. Within fifteen minutes of us returning back home, my mom's water broke and everyone went into an immediate panic. My dad was running around trying to get together Peter's luggage seeing that he would be staying with Simone's parents until my parents were back from the hospital. My mom was running around trying to gather her luggage and at the same time constantly apologizing for missing dinner. I told her that she didn't have to apologize for going into labor. I then wished her good luck and off they went to the hospital.

Nina entered this world within six hours. My mom had just giving birth to a healthy baby girl that had no signs of any complications. Everyone was surprised that Nina was born so fast. I was even making plans of returning back to home the following day after I was done with my classes. But there would be no need for that because I got the chance to see my little sister that same night.

It was now May 2004 and my freshmen year in college had gone by fast. From August 2003 until October 2003 I lived with Simone, Denise, and Eliza. From October 2003 until January 2004 I lived with Simone, Kimberly, and Amber. And from January 2004 until May 14, 2004 I lived with Amber, Lindsay, and Alexa. May 14, 2004 was the day that everyone said good-bye and headed back home for the summer. You'd think someone had died by the way that everyone was crying that afternoon.

I remember that me, Amber, Lindsay, Alexa, Belle, and two boys from next door by the names of Brett and David went out with us to dinner at Applebee's the night before and had a great time. And of course Applebee's was followed by a night of us partying like we were rock stars.

To all of our surprises, we all woke up early the next morning. We didn't have any food in the house because everything had to be cleared out the day before due to the fact that we were moving out.

So, Alexa, being the kind person that she is, bought all of us lunch from McDonalds. I don't know how much money she spent, but I do know that she bought food for me, her, Lindsay, Belle, David, Brett, and Chris John, another friend of ours. Alexa bought lunch for everyone except Amber. And that's because Amber only eats fruits, vegetables, and pizza. We all ate our food together as well as joking around about silly things that had happened that year, while music played in the background. Within an hour, we would all start to slowly disappear, one by one.

Alexa was the first one to leave out of us five girls. We all crowed around her crying gave her a hug and back to Whitehall, WI she went. Belle, who had chosen to stay until Friday with my roommates and I was the second one to leave. We did the same for Belle as we had done for Alexa, and back to Austin, MN she went. The third one to leave was Amber, and I must admit that I cried the hardest when she left. Amber and I had been through so much together, and now she was returning back to Fairmount, MN.

Lindsay and I were the last two left in our apartment. Lindsay and I had grown extremely close to each other once I moved into their apartment. So I also found it hard to say good-bye to her as well. I remember that we'd always joke around about us being long lost twin sisters minus the fact that I was Black and she was White, due to the fact that we were a lot alike in various ways. Lindsay and I chatted with the boys next door for a little and then it was time for her to go. We stood in the middle of the dorm parking lot crying and hugging each other at the same time. Then off she drove back to Marshfield, WI. I was the last one out of us five girls to leave.

My car had broken down at least six different times throughout my freshmen year in college, and just by chance it broke down again at the end of the school year. So my parents had to drive both of their vehicles to Rochester and help me move all of my belongings back home for the summer. This fact alone is why I was the last one to leave. I remember feeling bad because gas was pretty expensive at this time and they were driving both of their vehicles just to help me move. Not to mention the fact they also brought Peter and Nina with. But they didn't mind.

Both my mom and dad cars were packed with my belongings, mostly clothes, purses, and shoes. My dad drove his car with both Peter and Nina in the back seat. And my mom drove her car with me in the passenger seat. I remember my mom saying that she didn't mind driving to Rochester because this just meant that she would have two hours to blast her music, seeing that both Peter and Nina were riding with my dad. I also remember that I was still crying as we were driving back to home.

My crying made my mom very happy. She just laughed at me and told that "You'll see them all again in three months when school starts up again". And then she just smiled at me. See the thing was that even though I had been living with them for five years both my mom and dad had only seen me cry maybe three times. Why? Because I was always the first person to say that crying was a sign of weakness. It was at this point that I realized that crying wasn't a sign of weakness; it was a sign of being human.

Chapter 16

Home for the Summer

    May 17, 2004 was the first day that I returned back to work at the grocery store. Everyone that I used to work with greeted me warmly. I had made prior arrangements with the store manager to work in the deli department. I told her that I needed a lot of hours this summer and she totally understood. She then told me that she knew that I wouldn't be able to get a lot of hours working as a cashier but that I could have all the hours that I wanted if I went back to deli, so I agreed. I remember that the first day that I returned that everyone thought that I was still going to be cashiering and once I told them that I was going to be working in the deli; they just looked at me with disgust.

    I didn't know why then but I would soon find out that it was because the deli was the most hated department in the entire store. Mostly because of pity customer complaints and the fact that other departments thought that the deli worker didn't work as hard just because we didn't had a night shift manager like other department in the store. But in all reality we were hard workers. I worked in the deli from May 17, 2004 until August 13, 2004 and within these three months I made over Five thousand dollars and became really good friends with my fellow deli worker. I also managed to slice a piece of middle finger off while cleaning a meat slicer.

    It's kind of funny because my mom didn't think that I'd last that long working in the deli. She said that I was too much of a girly girl to be working in a deli. She was right. I found it extremely gross the first day that I started work. Everything from the smells of certain foods, the way certain foods were made, and worst of all the grease. Now don't get me wrong I love greasy food, especially the grocery store's Homemade fried chicken. But once you're around grease all day, it just does something to you. The worst thing of all was when I'd have to pour the dirty grease into buckets and then take it out to the back of the store to be recycled. This task by far was the worst. The smell of the grease made me gag each time.

But in the end it was all worth it. I say this because we all have to do certain things that we don't like or want to do, but once you're done you just feel that much better about yourself. I needed to make money during the summer and I knew that working hard was the only way that I was going to accomplish this, so I just did what needed to be done. The grocery store was all I'd known, I'd been working there for years before I went off to college so I knew that they'd welcome me back. Working in the deli was gross at times but it was also a great experience for me, and once again, an experience that I wouldn't trade it for anything else in the world.

Most of my summer was spent working the two in the afternoon until ten at night shift in the deli. But in my free time I hung out with my best friend Nichole and my godson Tommy, who she had just giving birth to on January 30, 2004. Nichole and I talked to each other once a week while I was in college, but once I got back home things weren't the same. We still talked to each other all the time, but one would think that since we only lived five blocks away from each other that we would hang out all the time. But this was the case. Nichole instead spent all of her time with her drug dealer boyfriend Steve, who I didn't care too much for.

Now I'm not going to sit her and be a hypocrite. I did like Steve in the beginning of May 2003 when I first met him. But this was mostly because he gave Nichole and I free weed all the time. But the second that Nichole told me that her laid a hand on her, I lost all respect for him. And the fact that Nichole chose to stay with him, made me lose a great deal of respect for her in a way as well. I remember the first time that Nichole called and told me that Steve had hit her but he said that he was sorry and that it wouldn't happen again. I told Nichole "If he's done it before, he'll do it again". And I was right.

Nichole told me that the first time Steve hit her was because someone said that he had complete control over her and when he asked Nichole if she thought that was true and she disagreed he smacked her in the face. But it was just a matter of time before the beatings would become more violent. One would involve him burning her with a cigarette, while another would involve them being in a hotel room and him choking her until she passed out, but the worst one of all would involve Steve telling Nichole to stay in the house and her disobeying his orders.

Everyone was fully aware that Steve indeed had complete control over Nichole. Whatever he told her to do she did. Expect one night that he told her to stay in the house. Nichole told me that she had been in the house all day and she wanted to go out for a little while. So she went over to one of her friend's house. She told me that she was standing outside smoking a cigarette when a car drove by and she noticed that Steve was inside. As the car turned around to come back Nichole dropped her cigarette told whoever she was standing outside with to tell Steve that she wasn't there and then she ran inside the house.

Telling Steve that Nichole wasn't there didn't do any good because he had already seen her. The plan was for Nichole to hide in the bathtub while another girl to pretend like she was using the bathroom, but this plan soon fell through as soon as Steve came busting through the bathroom door. He then began hitting Nichole in her face, he then grabbed her by her hair and drug her by her hair from the bathroom through the entire house all the way outside and then throw her into the car he had came in. Once inside the car Steve continued to push and choke Nichole until he felt that she had enough.

Nichole telling me this story just made me hate Steve even more as well as made me even more disgusted with her. I remember asking Nichole "What happened to the tough girl that I met back in 1999 that didn't take shit from anyone? What happened to the girl that was always the first one ready to fight whenever anything didn't go her way"? Nichole sat there in silence. She later told me that she was scared to hit him back and that she never would because he was the father of her baby.

I told Nichole "Regardless to the fact that he's the father of your baby. That still doesn't give him the right to ever lay a hand on you. What happens in he chokes you so bad that you black out and never wake back up. You getting away from him would be the best thing for you and your baby"!

I also went on to tell Nichole that I know that I'd never been in a situation like the one that she was in. I also told her that if I ever was, all it would take is for a guy to hit me once and that I would be out of there. I told her that there is no such thing as staying with a man that beats you for the sake of your child. But as you can guess all of my preaching didn't work. Instead I just sat there and listened to Nichole tell me how she was going to change her life around. I knew that Nichole would never change her lifestyle, just like I knew that she would never leave Steve because she "loved him" too much. But what could I do I was her friend. I had to support her even though we both knew that she wasn't doing what was best for her or her baby.

At this point in time Steve no longer beats Nichole on a frequent basis because he's always in and out of jail for numerous drug cases. And Nichole is looking at some prison time herself. Nichole has numerous drug cases pending against her not to mention the fact that she's gotten her house raided right along with her grandmother's. She's also looking at some prison time for stealing and then writing out over Five thousand of her grandmother's checks. This money was used to buy Steve two used cars so that he would be able to drive back and forth from Illinois to Minnesota with his drugs. But the cars didn't last long because Steve blew one up and his friend totaled the other in a car accident. Nichole also informed me of her plans to marry Steve and have three more children with him.

Whenever I wasn't counseling Nichole I'd hang out with my friend Jasmine. Jasmine was a girl that I had met my senior year in high school. She was a year younger than me but we still hung out occasionally and smoke pot together. It's kind of weird how Jasmine and I became close friends. She had started working at the grocery store in August 2003. This was around the time that I quite due to the fact that I was attending college in Rochester. I remember returning home one weekend and stopping by the grocery store and her saying that she hadn't seen me in awhile. I told her that Simone and I were both living in Rochester, and I invited her up to party with us.

Jasmine's first visit was in October 2003 and I was living in the apartment with Simone, Kimberly, and Amber. Now Jasmine was a friend of both Simone and I, and we partied together from October 2003 until January 2004. But once Simone and I went our separate ways, Jasmine still chose to drive to Rochester every weekend and hang out with me. It was at that point that Jasmine and I became very close friends. We both decided that we were going to be roommates once school started in August 2004.

It was now July 2004; I usually have a great memory when it comes to dates, but not in this case. All I remember is that I was working in the deli with my cell phone in my pocket. I always kept my cell phone in my pocket on vibrate. When all of a sudden my pocket began to vibrate, I took my phone out of my pocket and looked down to see who it was and it read "Grandpa Barry". I was extremely shocked to see the number on my phone seeing that the last time that I spoke to my grandfather or Beth was in June 2003 when they informed me that they wouldn't be attending my graduation ceremony due to my grandfather being sick. So of course I had to answer it.

I remember that I snuck back in a corner of the deli and answered my phone, but at the end of the conversation, I would wish that I hadn't. I answer my phone with "hello" the next thing I heard was Beth's voice. Her exact words to me were "Hello Timesha, this is Beth. I know we haven't spoken to each other in awhile and I hate that I have to call you with bad news. But Donald's dead".

I remember immediately dropping to my knees, as well as feeling nothing but guilt in my heart for not keeping in contact with Donald. I asked her what had happened and she told me that he had been shot numerous times by a police officer because they thought that he had stolen a car but in reality the car that he was driving was his. Beth told me that her and my grandfather were filing a lawsuit for wrongful death against the police department. She also told me that she would keep me posted as to what was going to happen. But she never did.

I remember going home from work that night and telling my parents about the phone call that I had received earlier that day. Both of my parents showed deep sympathy but I told them that I was fine. I then went upstairs and typed a letter to my grandfather and Beth explaining how there was no way possible that I knew what they we going through. But that I was also hurting as well even though I hadn't seen Donald in seven years or talked to him in four. I even had my dad photocopy a picture that I had found in my bedroom of Donald.

In the picture Donald looked so happy. And this brought tears to my eyes. Donald was standing in front of a birthday cake with a big smile on his face. I sent this picture along with the letter that I typed to them as well. The picture had to have been taken when Donald was ten or eleven years old, which would have made the picture at least twenty-two years old. And the weird thing is that I don't remember how I had gotten the picture. All I know is that I had moved from Illinois to Minnesota seven years ago, and through out those seven years, this picture some how stayed with me. I didn't even have a picture of Sperm, but I had one of my Uncle Donald. It made me sad to think that out of my grandfather's four sons, Donald was the only one that had chosen to clean up his life in return only to turn around and have to taken away at such a young age.

After I was done typing the letter and my dad had the picture photocopied for me, I just sat in the middle of my bedroom floor with many thoughts as well as memories racing through my head. I remembered that when I was younger that Donald used to play house with me, I remembered him driving to Brodview to bring me a stuffed animal and five dollars when Sperm stood me up, and I even remembered talking to Donald on the phone between the years of 1999 and 2000. I remember that 1999-2000 was around the time that Donald had told me that he had some kind of job that involved him traveling to different states and that if he ever came to Minnesota that we would hang out. We never got the chance to hang out back then. And now we never will.

Chapter 17

Lies, Lies, and More Lies

I waited for weeks to hear back from Grandpa Barry and Beth, but I never did. I even called their house and left them messages but they never returned my calls and after awhile I stopped reaching out to them because it was quite obvious that they didn't want anything to do with me. My Grandma Yolanda told me that she had spoken to both my grandfather and Beth and that they were doing a lot better. I felt somewhat relived hearing this from her, but it still didn't make sense to me why they couldn't pick up the phone for me, return my messages, or even pick up a pen and a piece of paper and at least have the decency to write me back. And that's when I realized that the love my grandfather once had for me was no longer there. And I continued on with my everyday life.

It was now July 2004 and I was now moving back to Rochester to attend my second year at RCTC in August once school started. I was extremely excited because I was going to be living in a house this year. But even more excited that I would only be living two minutes away from Amber, Lindsay, Alexa, Belle, and Sarah. The plan was for me, Jasmine, and a girl by the name of Karen, a girl that I had meet last school year to live together in this three-bedroom, two-bathroom house together. But that plan fail through due to the fact that Karen continued to make up different excuses whenever it came time for us to sign our leases. So just by chance David, the boy that lived next door to me last year was looking for a place to live and he agreed to be our roommate. The thought of me, Jasmine, and David living together sounded good at first but I knew deep inside that it wasn't going to work.

Jasmine and I were still close friends, but when it came to David that was a different story. David and I had met each other back in August 2003 and he was my best guy friend. He'd come grocery shopping with me, clothes shopping with me, give me free weed, take me out to dinner, and as time passed by he would even start buying me jewelry. I must admit that I thought David was gay at first because he really didn't try "getting on me" as most guys in his situation would have done. But I didn't mind if David was gay because one of my dad's brothers is gay, plus I always wanted a gay friend. But as time passed by David would try "getting on me" on many occasions and one day towards the end of February, I gave in.

David would be the one and only guy that I'd have sex with from April 2004 until August 2004 and each time he'd tell me that he was becoming more and more attached to me. At first I didn't care, sex was sex to me; all I wanted to do was get off. As time passed by I would begin to start having feeling for David but they wouldn't last long do the fact that he was a compulsive liar that craved for attention. David was the type of person that no matter who you were talking to or what you were talking about, he'd always find so kind of bizarre way to tie himself into the story. He lied so much that each time he told me something I'd have to ask him "Now give me one good reason why I should believe what you're telling me is the truth".

By the time July rolled around I made it very clear to David that I didn't want anything to do with him. I told him that we just really liked this house and needed a third roommate. I also told David he should be prepared for me bringing guys home and having them stay them night. And I remember him telling me "You can bring as many guys home as you want. I really don't care. I do know that I won't be bringing any other girls home". He also told me "Timesha it could be ten years from now and you can have seven kids with seven different men and I'd still want to be with you". It was at this point that I realized that the only reason why David had agreed to be our roommate was that he somehow thought that us living in the same household would somehow bring us closer together.

August 2004 was the first time that I had sex with another guy other than David. Of course he found out, and one would think that he would no longer be interested in me. But this wasn't the case, David was under the impression that I still wanted to be with him and that the only reason why I had slept with another guy was to try and make him no longer want to be with me. This was far from the truth; I'd had sex with another guy simply because I wanted to. It had nothing to do with David in any way, shape, or form. And even if that were my plan it wouldn't have worked, because after David found out about what I had done, he still wanted to be with me. It was at this point that I realized that David was just going through a faze and in do time he'd get over me.

Although David had now signed a lease and was soon to be living with Jasmine and I, he really wasn't around that often. I remember that he would always lie about bringing a television he had to our new house so that we could use it in our living room. David must have lied to us about the television at least three weeks in a role. So Jasmine and I decided to tell him that we were driving up to Andover, MN where he lived to get it. On the day that we were suppose to go, David refused to answer the phone for us. This was the last straw for me because there is nothing more that I hate than being lied to.

So the next time that I got a hold of David I exploded. I told him that I thought he was a compulsive liar and the he needed to seek professional help fast. I also remember saying to him "Imagine how long your nose would be if it grew an inch each time you lied, pretty long huh". I even went, as far as to say that I didn't believe that his father was really dead. Back in July, I had told David that my Uncle Donald had passed away. And the next week, David called me up telling me that his dad who he claims lived in Jamaica and was also part owner of a Sandals Resort hotel, had gotten in a car accident along with David's half sister and his grandmother. According to David, his dad was driving around a sharp turn in Jamaica with David's little sister and his grandmother in the car as well, when they were struck by a semi truck. David told me that his father had died along with his grandmother but that his little sister had survived.

I must admit that the timing was kind of odd, but I believed David at first. That is until he really didn't seem to care when I told him that he had made up the story about his father and grandmother passing away. The way he responded to me telling him this wasn't the way that a normal person would've responded. Once I told David that I didn't believe that his father and grandmother had passed away his exact words to me were "O.k. Timesha". O.k. Timesha wasn't the response that I was looking for. Because I know damn well that if my father and my grandmother had just passed away I'd sure as hell have a lot more to say than "O.k. Timesha".

It was just a matter of time before me; Jasmine, and everyone else would realize how much of a liar David truly was. It was the end of August, when David called our landlord and told him that he was leaving for Jamaica and that he wouldn't be back until January 2005. David claimed that he was going to Jamaica to handle his father's affairs. It was at this time that David told our landlord that he still wanted to stay on the lease and that he would send Jasmine and I a check in the mail each month to cover his share of the rent. Jasmine and I really didn't mind nor care seeing that the two of us had been living in the house for two months by ourselves. Within that two months David stopped by maybe twice, but each time he always forgot to bring the television.

So David told everyone that he and his family were going to Jamaica until January to handle his father's affairs. Right! So that would explain why when Amber called his house in October his brother answered the phone and told her that David wasn't home. When Amber asked where he was, his brother replied, "He joined the Army." I also found out that David had told numerous of people that the reason that he wouldn't be attending school first semester was because he would be in Jamaica handling his father's affairs. That was another lie. The reason why David wouldn't be attending school first semester was because he was kicked out of school for plagiarizing.

The reason that I know for a fact that David was kicked out of school for plagiarizing was because he told me himself. Now everyone knew that David really isn't a reliable source, so that's when Amber comes into play. Amber and David had been in a Psychology class together back in April 2004, when one day, their teacher announced that someone in the class had plagiarized. David told Amber right then and there that he was the person that the teacher was talking about. And he was right, the teacher told David that she knew that he had plagiarized and he pretty much stopped going to school after that. This my friend's is the real reason why David wouldn't be attending school first nor second semester.

It was now September 7, 2004 and I was no longer known as Timesha Ge'na Mullins. I was now Timesha Ge'na Mohan. And even though both my parents had always treated me like I was their own child, it just felt that much better to have the same last name as them. It gave me a sense of belonging. I'd had the name Mullins for nineteen years. But it meant nothing to me. Mullins was just a constant reminder of me trying to be a part of a family that wanted nothing to do with me. But Mohan on the other hand, now that meant something to me. I had been contemplating the idea of a name change for years, and in the summer of 2004 I went to the County Courthouse and got the papers for the name change.

I must admit that changing my last name was a big hassle, but in the end it was all worth it. Kelly and Bryan were my new family now, they had done so many great things for me through the five years that I had been living with them. So I saw me changing my last name as a way to pay tribute to them. I remember that the judge asked me why I wanted to change my last name, and I stood up right in front of my mom, my dad, Peter, Nina, and the entire courtroom and said "The last name Mullins means nothing to me, nor has it brought me any good. This has been my only family for the past five years, and it would make me feel more like I was apart of the family if I had the same last name as them".

That was it, my family and celebrated the event of my name change by going out for Chinese food, and the following week, I had papers to prove that I was Timesha Ge'na Mohan. I knew in my heart that I had done the right thing. Many people told me that it was a smart move on my part. My Grandma Yolanda even gave me her support by telling me "You did the right thing Timesha! Kelly and Bryan have been nothing but good to you for so many years! And I'm proud of you for doing it"! This is the complete opposite reaction that Egg would have once she found out.

Chapter 18
Think Before You Speak

By the time the end of September came around everyone would realize for the last time how much of a liar David truly was. It was also at this time that David must have got wind that his brother had told Amber that he had joined the Army. Which is why I'm more that sure is the reason why he called me. Jasmine nor I or anyone else had heard from David in three months. But we really didn't care as long as the checks for his part of the rent kept coming in the mail. David by now knew that I wanted absolutely nothing to do with him, so he didn't call me from his cell phone fully aware that I wouldn't answer it. Instead David called me from a 312 number. I answer the number because I was fully aware to the fact that 312 numbers are from the Chicago area and I figured that it was one of my family members. Wrong! It was David. And can you believe that this boy had the nerve to try and lie to me by telling me that he wasn't in Chicago. That's when I replied to Joey "Are you really gonna sit here and try and tell me that I'm lying? Do you not realize how many of my family members have 312 numbers? You might not be in Chicago, but your somewhere in the area".

The entire conversation was pointless. All David talked about was us being together, and when I asked him if he was supposed to be in Jamaica, then why was he calling me from Illinois. His only response was "I'm taking care of business". What business could David possible have been taking care of? We're taking about an eighteen-year-old boy that had never even had a job in his entire life. But now all of a sudden he's in Illinois "taking care of business". David would soon begin to call me from many weird numbers and I'd always answer simply because it was an odd number and I was curious to see who it was. Between November and December David would call and tell me that he was in Illinois, Texas, Florida, Arizona, and many other states. And when I'd ask him what he was doing he'd always say, "taking care of business".

Once David realized how much I truly disliked him, he then took it upon himself to tell Amber and Belle that once he moved back to Rochester in January, he wasn't going to live with Jasmine and I. David told both Amber and Belle that he was coming to Rochester on December 19th and that he was going to look for an apartment and also buy furniture for his apartment. To make a long story short, I'll just tell you now. David never came to Rochester, MN on December 19th. And to this day, no one has heard from him since.

So as far as I'm concerned, David never went to Jamaica if he was calling my friends and I from Illinois, Texas, Arizona, and Florida between September and December when he was suppose to be in Jamaica until January 2005. And I sure as hell don't believe that his father and grandmother died in a car accident. I told David once before, and I'll tell him again "the only way that I'll believe that you dad and grandmother died in a car accident is if you show me their obituaries"!

November 3, 2004 the day before the Bush VS. Kerry election is the day that Amber and I met Josh Hartnett. For those of you who don't know who Josh Hartnett is, let me enlighten you. Josh Hartnett who by the way is from Minnesota, has starred in many movies such as "Black Hawk Down", "O", "40 days and 40 nights", and of course his latest movie "Wicker Park". I will never forget, it was around two o'clock in the afternoon when Amber and I were walking from our English class. When a guy that I didn't know approached us and asked us if we knew who Josh Hartnett was. Of course we knew who Josh Hartnett, what kind of question was that.

We then told him "yes" and that's when he told us that Josh Hartnett would be arriving at our school in ten minutes. I must admit that me along with a lot of other people didn't believe him, but we decide to stick around anyway. At this exact same time I noticed that there were two people who I assumed we from the newspaper because they had a large camera with them. That's when I told Amber that they were there to take pictures of Josh Hartnett and that I was going to ask them if they'd take a picture of me with him once he got there. I then we over and asked the lady and gentleman who I assumed worked for a newspaper company, if they were they to take pictures of Josh Hartnett and believe it or not, the didn't even know who Josh Hartnett was or that he was coming. They then told me that they were at my school to do a survey on the up coming election and asked me if I wanted to do the survey and I told them "sure"

The survey consisted of them saying a word that related to the election and me telling them the first thing thought that came to my mind. After the survey the newspaper reporters from the Post Bulletin disappeared, and Amber and I, who had been standing there for fifteen minutes waiting for Josh Hartnett continued to wait. Within minutes the lady and gentleman from the Post Bulletin returned and asked me if I would rather be in their "Weekly Fashion" section, and once again I told them "sure". I then stood in the middle of the atrium, as they told me to, so that they could take pictures of me. When all of a sudden a lot of people began to crowd around me. At least I though that it was me they were crowding, but in reality, they were only crowding around me because I was standing right next to Josh Hartnett.

Yep, Josh Hartnett had walked in without me or the newspaper reporters even noticing. Once the three of us realized he was there, we immediately focused our attention on him to find out why he was at our school. And I should have known that the only reason why Josh Hartnett was only at our school to try and persuade everyone to vote for John Kerry. We all know that in the end his surprise visit as well as his speech didn't help Kerry win the election. Josh Hartnett was only at our school for about seven minutes, and as fast as he arrived, he took off even faster. But before he left he did do Amber and I the honor of signing his autograph on two "Vote for John Kerry/Edwards" posters for us. Needless to say, Jolene as well as all of Amber's roommates were extremely jealous that we got to meet Josh Hartnett.

Thursday, November 17, 2004 was the day that I became "The talk of the Town" all over again. I woke up that morning fully aware that I was going to be in Post Bulletin's Weekly fashion section. The women who had taken my picture and given me my interview over the phone had told me the exact day that I was to be in the paper. Plus I had to go out and buy numerous copies. One for me, one for Kelly's parents, one for Bryan's mom, one for my mom to hang up at work, and of course one for both of my parents to keep at home.

But of course that morning I got up and pretended like I didn't know that I was in the paper. This really didn't work out that well. I had numerous teachers and students congratulating me throughout the entire day. Not to mention the fact that my math teacher had clipped the article out of the newspaper and gave it to me in class. I thought that was extremely cute, but I must admit that I was a little embarrassed as well. The superintendent would also show his support as well by clipping the article out of the newspaper and mailing it to my parents with a hand written letter congratulating me as well as telling me "It's always wonderful to see our student's great success throughout the year". I was happy and so were my parents, it was like my senior year in high school all over again.

November 17, 2004 was also the day that Egg would find out that I had changed my last name. I hadn't spoken to Egg in well over six months. But that was by choice. Egg would call me numerous of times but I would never answer for her. I remember that it got to the point that I wouldn't even answer my cell phone to any numbers that began with 651. 651 is the area code in the St. Paul area of Minnesota, which is where Egg lived. It wasn't that I was afraid to talk to Egg. It was just that I didn't have the time or energy to talk to Egg. Besides she never had anything worth wild to talk about anyway. All she'd do is bitch about Suzanne violating her legal parental rights by not allowing her to speak to the boys and this would always be followed by her begging me to come and visit her in St. Paul because according to her, I was all she had left.

When in reality, it wasn't that Suzanne wasn't allowing Mitchell and Jacob to talk to Egg; it was the simple fact that they didn't want to talk to Egg. As for me, by the time 2003 and 2004 came around gas prices were high, and my rent wasn't getting any cheaper. So I told Egg that unless she was going to reimburse me for the money that I would be losing by taking off time from work to come and visit her that she could forget about it. And as of today, I've yet to go and visit Egg in St. Paul.

Now, the way that Egg found out that I had changed my last name is kind of a funny story. I'm assuming that Egg called my phone one day and got to hear my new voice mail, which said, "You have reached Timesha Mohan leave a message". And according to my Grandma Yolanda, she went crazy. My grandmother and I talk to each other one a week sometimes twice. But I remember on this particular night that I called her. The first thing that she said to me was "Have you talked to your mama lately"? And I responded "no". This is when Grandma Yolanda then informed me that she had. She told me that Egg had called her the night before bitching up a storm about me being a stupid Bitch. The reason behind me being a stupid Bitch was the simple fact that I had changed my last name. This is what Egg had said according to Grandma Yolanda. "That stupid Bitch Timesha doesn't know how bad she just fucked herself over! Now she's not going to get any money when Barry (Grandpa Barry) dies"!

I just laughed, and now I had even more of a reason not to talk to Egg. Grandma Yolanda then told me that she had told Egg that she thought that I had done the right thing. My grandmother said that she told Egg "I don't think that she did anything wrong by changing her name. Kelly and Bryan have always been there for her! Where was Barry all those damn years when she needed him"? But my grandfather being there when I needed him was the last thing that Egg was concerned about. The only thing she was concerned about was who all his money would go to once he died. And this fact alone made me dislike her even more.

Here I had done a something that was good in everyone else eyes, only to have her try and bring me down. Of course I knew that she wasn't going to be happy about me changing my name, but I really didn't care. I had all the support that I needed from all of the people that I loved. But the last thing that I would have expected her to do was to pretty much wish death upon my grandfather just because of me changing my last name.

Chapter 19
The Call

November 23rd just two days before Thanksgiving was the first time that I had talked to Sperm in five years. Once again, I had been talking to Grandma Yolanda and she had told me that had spoken to Grandpa Barry and Beth. I'm assuming that Sperm was around as well. Grandma Yolanda told me that he had asked her for my phone number because he wanted to talk to me. She said that she didn't feel comfortable giving it to him without my permission. So, instead, she wrote down his phone number and told him that she would give it to me and tell me that Sperm want to speak to me. She also told him that it would be up to me to give him a call. I thanked my grandmother for not giving out my phone number.

I then wrote down Sperm's number, told my grandmother that I loved her, wished her good-night, and then I must have sat on my couch for at least an hour and half debating on whether or not I was going to call Sperm. I was torn. In one way I wanted to talk to Sperm, but in another way I didn't. That's when I decided to call the one person that I knew could help me make the right decision, my mom. I called and told her that I had just got done talking to my grandmother and that she had told me that Sperm want to talk to me. I also told her that my grandmother had given me Sperm's phone number and asked her if I should call him or not.

My mom then told me that it wasn't up to her as to whether or not I should call Sperm. She told me that that would be a choice that I would have to make that decision on my own. She also told me that she didn't think that it would be such a bad idea to call him seeing that I hadn't spoke to him in a long time, and that maybe he something important that he wanted to tell me. It was at this point that I had heard enough and I decided to call Sperm. I picked up my cell phone and dialed the ten-digit number that my grandmother had given me. A woman answered the phone and she had a sense of irritation in her voice when she said "Hello". I then asked her if Kevin was home. The woman then told me that he was there and for me to hold on a second and that she would go and get him.

I sat on the other end of the line with my heart beating fast. It was at that time when I heard Sperm's voice in the background. He was asking the woman if she knew who was on the phone and she told him that she didn't know. Although I hadn't seen or talked to him in five years, I could still recognize his voice. The sound of his voice made a lump form in my throat. The sound of his voice also sent chills through my body and almost made me hang up the phone. It had been five years. I was scared and I didn't know what I was supposed to say to him. But most of all I had the fear of him not remembering me. What if I said, "Hi, this is Timesha"? And he responded "Timesha who"? I couldn't bare the thought of my biological father not remembering that he had a daughter. I'd had enough I was hanging up. But just as I pulled the phone away from my ear, I heard an all too formal "Hello".

It was Sperm. All of a sudden I felt like a little girl all over again. No matter how much Sperm had lied to me when I was younger I always forgave him. The reason why I believe that I always forgave him was because he was never around when I was growing up. This is why what few memories that I have of him are all good. I always remember him being happy to see me, always taking me out to eat, always giving me money, never using foul language towards me, and never once laying a hand on me. But my memories were the complete opposite when it came to Egg. And this is the only reason why I believe that I have stronger feeling for Sperm than Egg. Because he wasn't around while I was growing up to cause me as much pain as Egg had done. I realize that in reality I should have harsher feeling towards Sperm than Egg seeing that she did the right thing trying to raise me while he just took off. But I don't. And I can't help the way that I feel.

Sperm answered the phone and to my surprise he remembered who I was. He also told me that the woman that had answered the phone was my Aunt Donna. We then talked to each other for about ten minutes. We tried our best to catch up on lost time. We talked mostly about my new family, me graduating high school, me attending my second year in college and so on. I was also amazed to the fact that Sperm cared enough to ask me how Egg and my brothers were doing. I told him that my brothers and I had been separated but that they were doing fine. And as for Egg I told him that I had no clue as too how or what she was doing, and that I hadn't talked to her in months.

My conversation with Sperm was extremely awkward, but I felt good about calling him once it was all over. But of course you know that our conversation couldn't end with him telling me that "Maybe me and your granddad can drive the Cadillac or Lexus up there and visit you some time next month"! I was fully aware that this was yet another one of Sperm's famous lies about coming to visit me. The only difference is that this time around I wouldn't have to cry myself to sleep as I waited for him to arrive. I knew that if we were ever going to see each other again, that I would have to be the one to make a trip back to Illinois. In due time, I would be making a trip back to Illinois. This trip would have nothing to do with Sperm. This trip is one that I would have much rather not taken, but yet a trip that I needed to take.

Chapter 20
Never Doubt Your First Instinct

The night of December 2, 2004 is a night that I will never forget. The night started out great. I remember that Jasmine and I had cooked dinner that night. It was around six o'clock in the evening and we had just gotten done eating fried pork chops, baked chicken, chicken rice-a-roni, and green beans. December 2nd was a Thursday night so of course dinner was going to be followed by a couple of alcoholic beverages. Each Thursday, also known, as "Thirsty Thursday" is the night when all college kids get totally trashed just because Thursday sounds like a good day to do so. This Thursday, I had already made previous plans to go and drink with one of my friend's Heather. Heather was a girl that I had met last year and she only lived about five minutes away from my house. Jasmine had plans as well. She would be hanging out with her cousins that evening.

So I redid my make-up and it must have been around a quarter after seven when I arrived at Heather's house. My new drink of choice was Gin. So, I brought along a liter of Gin as well as a couple of beers and poured myself a glass of Gin and orange juice right away. Me, Heather, and a couple of her roommates sat and watched television and drank. I remember that when I had first gotten to Heather's house I was pumped to get drunk. But as time passed by I really didn't feel like drinking anymore. I remember that Heather even asked me why I wasn't drinking, and I told her "You know I have to drink slowly otherwise I'll end up hovered over your bathroom toilet"! She just laughed. Everyone knew that I was a lightweight. I was also known for getting drunk and passing out in random bathrooms. But I guess deep down inside, I knew that something terrible was going to happen, and I didn't want to be completely trashed when it did.

By now it was a little after eight o'clock when my phone rang. It was Simone. Simone told me that she was hanging out in at home and that there was nothing to do. She then asked me what I was doing and I told her getting drunk and she asked me if it was alright if her and two other girls from came up to Rochester and get drunk with me. I then muted my phone and asked Heather if it was alright if Simone came up and she said that was fine. I then told Simone that they could come up and she told me that she would see me in about an hour. It was now an hour since I had poured my drink and I still hadn't finished it. To my surprise no one even noticed that I was still on my first drink, because if they had known I'm sure I would've poked fun at me.

Simone and her two friends arrived to Heather's house at about a quarter after nine. We all talked, listened to music, and were making plans to go over to the dorms once we were really drunk and hang out with some of the freshmen. I even told Simone that our very first roommate from last year, Eliza, still lived out there in the exact same apartment. Simone got a kick out of this and told me that she was going to go and visit Eliza and see if she remembered her. I told Simone that she would because she had remembered me. Everyone was joking around and having a great time. It was a little before nine thirty when I finally finished my drink. Little did I know that within a matter of minutes that I was going to receive a phone call that would forever change my life.

I will never forget that it was nine thirty six when my phone rang. I looked down at my phone to see who it was and it read "Grandma Yolanda". Simone then asked me who it was and I told her that it was my grandma. She then told me to tell her that she said "Hi" and I told her that I would. Simone and my grandmother had met each other at my graduation party the year before. I then said "Why is she calling me so late, she's usually asleep by now"! Then I answered the phone jokingly saying "What are you doing up so late? Isn't past your bedtime grandma"? And her exact words to me were "Timesha, I got some bad news to tell you. Grandma Mrs. Rolland just died a couple of hours ago". And my heart dropped. It was at this point that I got up off the couch and moved from the living room to the upstairs bathroom so that I could hear what had happen.

As I sat alone in the bathroom trying to grasp the fact that the only great grand mother that I had ever had as well as ever known was now dead, it hit me. It all made sense why I hadn't been able to get drunk that night. My grandmother's death was the reason why I had a gut feeling that something terrible was going to happen that night. To this day, I'm glad that I didn't get drunk that night; otherwise, I don't think that I would have been able to forgive myself.

I sat in the bathroom talking to Grandma Yolanda and she told me that at this point she really wasn't sure how Grandma Mrs. Rolland had passed away. The only thing that she could tell me was that she was for sure dead because her and my cousin Tommy (Uncle Ernest James son) had viewed her body that night. She also informed me that Auntie Ellen's husband Otis, along with their son Wes had gone to view the body before her and Tommy had and that once they were done then the decided to call my Grandma and tell her that her mother was dead. Otis had decided that he wasn't going to tell Auntie Ellen that Grandma Mrs. Rolland was dead because it would be too much for her to handle. And as for Uncle Ernest James, no one had the slightest clue as to where he was. Grandma Yolanda told me that both her and Wes had people out looking for him to tell him what had happen, but no one could find him.

It was at this point that Grandma Yolanda asked me if I knew or anyway to get ahold of Egg and I told her "No". This was the one and only time that I had ever felt bad about not keeping in contact with Egg. Here I was talking to my grandma on the phone, and she's telling me that her mother just passed away, and I couldn't even give her a phone number so that she could call and tell Egg what had happened. She then told me that she had a number written down that Egg had given to her the last time that they talked and that she was going to call and see if Egg was there. I then told Grandma Yolanda try and get ahold of Egg and that once she was done talking to Egg that she should try and get some rest. I told

Grandma Yolanda not to worry because Grandma Mrs. Rolland was in a better place now and that things would be alright. I also told Grandma Yolanda that I didn't have a lot of money at that time because I had just got done paying my rent, but that I would somehow find a way to get back to Illinois.

I didn't know what to say to her. Here she had just lost her mother and I was fully aware that there was nothing that I could say that was going to change that. I go off the phone and I walked downstairs. I didn't feel like partying anymore so I told everyone that I was going home. Just as I walked outside of Heather's house and hopped into my car, my phone rang. I looked down and I saw that it was a 651 number. I knew that it was Egg, and for the first time in over nine months, I answered.

I hadn't talked to Egg in nearly nine months, and the last thing that I expected for us to be talking about was the death of our grandmother. But yet we were, and it wasn't by choice. Egg was crying as I was talking to her, now usually I wouldn't pay her crying much attention because I've known her for years and I know that she fakes crying to get attention. But on this night I actually felt her pain. I knew that I was hurting and I had only know Grandma Mrs. Rolland for twelve years, six of which I spend almost everyday with her. Then Egg surely must have been hurting as well. She would be turning forty-three in just six days, and had known Grandma Mrs. Rolland all of her life. I was even told by varies members of my family that Grandma Mrs. Rolland had owned a restaurant before I was born, and that she named it after Egg.

But whatever feeling of sympathy that I had for Egg quickly vanished once she brought up my name change. Her exact words to me were "Timesha, can I ask you a question?" I replied, "Yes". "Did you recently get married"? Asked Egg. I replied "No, why". "Because I called your phone awhile back and you said a different last name". Replied Egg. "Yeah I know. I got my last name changed a couple of months ago, to Mohan. The last name of my family" I replied. "Oh" replied Egg. "Timesha do you really hate me that much? Because you know that I tried my best, you of all people should know that no one's perfect!" stated Egg. I had no clue as to what the hell she was referring to with her "you of all people" comment. But I didn't hesitate to remind her that I was no longer a fourteen-year-old girl, and that I was a grown woman. "First of all this is not the time to talking about any of your problems. We have bigger issues to deal with here. Don't you realize that Grandma Mrs. Rolland just died"? Of course Egg realized that Grandma Mrs. Rolland had just died, but even then, she still couldn't and wouldn't take out the time to think about anybody other than herself.

I then told Egg that I had spoken with Sperm a couple of weeks ago. But she didn't care the first words out of her mouth were "What did that sorry ass bitch have to say"? I replied, "We actually had a good conversation and he was just wondering how you and the boys were doing". "He knows damn well that he doesn't care how the boys are doing" Egg stated. And I replied, "Well I still thought that it was nice of him to ask"!

It was at this point that our conversation quickly came to an end. I told Egg that I could no longer talk to her anymore and that I would call her back sometime tomorrow. I then called my parents to tell them what had happen. My mom answered and she told me that she was so sad to hear what had happened. She then asked me what I was planning on doing since my great grandmother had just passed away. And I replied "I wanna got back to Illinois to see her one last time, but I don't have any money, and my car probably won't make it". My mom then replied "I don't blame you for wanting to go back to Illinois. I'd do the same thing if me grandmother died. And I'll transfer money into your checking account the first thing tomorrow morning. But the first thing you'll have to do is call the train station and let me know how much a two-way ticket is going to cost".

I thanked my mom very much for loaning me even more money. In a way I felt bad because at this point in time I already owed my parents nearly four thousand dollars. The money that I owed my parents was due to all the work I had done on my car. It was everything from two new engines, a new car starter, a new radiator, new tires, new shocks, new shrug, new brakes, alignment, you name, and guarantee it's been fixed. The only thing that I can honestly say that hasn't broken down yet is the transmission. But I know that that's going to the next thing to go. But this time I know that my mom honestly didn't even mind borrowing me money.

139

I thanked my mom again for borrowing me money. She told me that it was fine and asked me if I was alright and if I wanted to talk about my grandmother passing away. I told her that I was fine and that I didn't want to talk about my grandmother's passing. So of course she tried sparking up a random conversation, but no matter what we tried talking about I'd somehow through in a comment about my grandmother. After awhile I got tired of planning the "Let's pretend like everything's okay game", and told my mom that I was going to bed and that I'd call her in the morning once I found out how much the train ticket was going to cost. She agreed, and I know deep down inside that she knew the real reason why I didn't want to talk to her anymore. I was in too much pain to talk about anything or anyone. I just needed to be alone.

After I got off the phone with my mom, I once again found myself sitting in the middle of my bedroom floor with many thoughts as well as memories racing through my head. I remembered that Grandma Mrs. Rolland didn't drink or smoke, I remembered that her favorite candy bar was a Baby Ruth, I remembered that while Egg was in the hospital giving birth to Mitchell that Grandma Mrs. Rolland made me breakfast that consisted of a bowl of Kix cereal with warm milk and then watched me from her window run right up the street to school, I remembered that we'd always watch "The Price Is Right, "People's Court", and "Wheel of Fortune" together, I remembered that I always loved to eat her famous homemade Vanilla Ice Cream as well as her Black eyed peas with ham hocks and sweet potato pie, I remembered that she would always bring me to church with her on Sundays anytime that I wanted to go, and I remembered that she and I used to sit outside during the summer in lawn chairs and sell peanuts for her church.

But most of all, I remembered that between the ages of nine and eleven that I used to sleep right next to her on the left hand side of her bed. I basically lived with her my last two years in Illinois, besides the month that Egg moved my brothers and I to Chicago right before we moved to Minnesota. Grandma Mrs. Rolland stayed exactly one block away from the elementary school that I attended and allowed me to live with her once Grandma Yolanda and my cousins moved to Maywood, IL, simply because I didn't want to switch schools and she loved me enough to let me live with her.

This is a woman that was very much involved in my life for the last six years that I had lived in Illinois and now I had to face the fact that she was gone. I sat in the middle of my bedroom floor with many thoughts as well as memories racing through my head. These wonderful thoughts and memories almost brought tears to my eyes. But due to the fact that I was not able to grasp the fact that Grandma Mrs. Rolland was actually gone, I wouldn't allow those tears to fall.

Chapter 21

The Morning Reality Struck

I woke up the next morning still in disbelief of the phone call that I had received from my Grandma Yolanda the night before. The first thing I did was grabbed a phone book off of my living room table and called the Amtrak train station. The lady that answered the phone at the Amtrak train station was extremely nice. She told me that the price for a two-way ticket would cost a little over one hundred dollars and that the nearest town that I could catch the train from was Winona, because the train didn't run though Rochester. She then asked me when I would be leaving as well as when I would be returning. I told her that I would be leaving on Sunday December 5th and retuning on Wednesday December 8th. I then told her that I wouldn't be arriving to Winona until Saturday evening and that I would pick up my ticket then, and she told me that would be fine.

I then called my mom right away and told how much the ticket was going to cost. She told me that it was a lot cheaper than what she had expected and that she would also put in some extra spending money for me to have since I'd be gone for three days. I then thanked her again and told her that I had to call my grandma and get ready for school but that I would call her later. I then called my grandma and she told me that she was doing alright and that she and Tommy were on their way down to the funeral home to discuss the funeral arrangements. I told her that I would be arriving in town of Sunday. I told her that I would call her later that night once I was done with work. I had to get to school and she had to get to the funeral home. We both agreed that we'd talk to each other later.

Next, I decided to call Egg. The night before Egg had been talking about going back to Illinois and that maybe we could go together. So, I called to let her know that I had just got done booking myself a train ticket. I also informed her that I was leaving for Illinois on Sunday and returning on Wednesday, I couldn't stay longer than that due to the end of my semester quickly approaching, not to mention the three finals that I had starting on Friday. I told her that would give them six days and they should have the funeral arrangements together by then. Egg then told me that she didn't know how or when she would be coming to Illinois because she didn't have any money. I then told her that I was just calling to let her know when I would be leaving and that I had to go otherwise I was going to be late for school.

I then got off the phone with Egg and decided that I was going to call Suzanne and Robert to inform them of my grandmother as well as my brother's grandmother passing away. It was after nine o'clock in the morning, and just as I had expected, no one answered the phone so I decided to leave a message. "Hi, Suzanne and Robert. This is Timesha and I was just calling to let you guys know that our great grandmother died last night. Both Katherine and I will be returning back to Illinois to attend her funeral. But the reason why I was calling was to let you know what had happened and I also wanted to leave it up to you as too whether or not you wanted to tell Mitchell and Jacob about it. I don't think that Jacob would remember her, but I do know that Mitchell would remember her for sure. So if you could please give me a call back, that would be great. Thanks a lot bye". This was the message that I left on the Hill's voicemail.

I had spent my entire morning making important phone calls and now it was less than a half an hour before my ten o'clock class started. I then brushed my teeth, threw on a pair of jeans along with a hoodie, grabbed my backpack, and off I went to school. No shower, no make-up, no nothing. This was the first time that anyone had ever seen me so plain before. I was always the person that got up two hours before class to get ready. I was always the person that jokingly said "First impressions last forever, so I have to look my best at all times. Plus I never know, today might be the day that I meet my future husband"! But on December 3rd I could have gave a rat's ass less what I looked like. I had bigger things to worry about other than whether or not today was going to be the day that I would meet my future husband.

I remember arriving to school that day and that a couple of people made a few comments about me being "dressed down" instead of "dressed up", and I just told them that I'd had a rough night. I really didn't feel like telling anyone that my grandmother had passed away because I really wasn't in the mood to have people telling me that they were so sorry to hear about my lost. Before I left for Illinois I probably told a total of thirteen people what had happen and how long that I would be gone. And that's only because I had too. This list of thirteen people included both of my parents, three of my teachers, my boss at work, Amber, Lindsay, Alexa, Belle, Nichole, and of course the message that I had left one Suzanne and Robert voicemail. I hadn't even seen Jasmine since we had eaten dinner together the night before, so I didn't even tell her what had happened or that I was leaving.

The first class of the day that I had was Sociology with Mr. Anderson. After class I told him that I wouldn't be attending class until next Friday due to my grandmother's passing away. Sociology was a Monday, Wednesday, Friday class, and I told him that I was leaving Sunday morning and that wouldn't be returning until Wednesday evening around eight o'clock in the evening. This was the first time since me finding out that my grandmother had died, that I had actually listened to the words that were coming out of my mouth. "My grandmother died last night and I have to go to Illinois to attend her funeral". It was at this point that I had finally came to accept the fact that my grandmother was truly gone. And I broke down in tears.

I stood right next to Mr. Anderson in front of a classroom that maybe five students were in and I cried. Mr. Anderson then gave me a warm hug and told me that it would be okay and not to worry because we were only going to be watching a movie for the two days that I would miss class. My other two teachers as well as my boss at work, all told me the same thing. It would be okay and that I wouldn't miss much in class or at work. As I stood in front of Mr. Anderson on December 3, 2004, I then realized that was the first time that I'd cried in seven months.

Chapter 22

Dear Mitchell and Jacob

It was now Sunday, December 5, 2004 and within a matter of minutes I would be leaving with my mom and heading to the train station. I had gotten up early that morning and my dad had made a huge breakfast for the family. We pretty much ate in silence. However my dad did ask me if I was excited to return back to Illinois due to the fact that I hadn't seen any of my family member besides my Grandma Yolanda in seven years. I told him that I was excited too see my four cousins of whom I'd grown up with. But I also added that it would be a lot more comfortable if it were under different circumstances, as to why I was retuning back to Illinois. My mom then asked me if I had heard back form Suzanne or Robert and I told her "No"

I really hadn't thought much about the voicemail that I had left for Suzanne and Robert just two days before. Although I was fully aware that they had indeed received my message. But once again I didn't think anything of it. That is until the day I was to leave for Illinois and my mom brought it up. Out of all the hundreds of messages that I'd left on their voicemail within the last five years, this is the only message that they didn't return. My mom the replied "I think that it's rather rude as well as inconsiderate of them not to have called you back". I looked across the table and replied, "Well I guess so". Then she replied "I thought that it was rather respectful of you to call and tell them what happened and leave it up to them as to whether or not they wanted to tell the boys. Because you could have just as easily called and asked to talk to Mitchell and told right then and there". She also added "But even more so, the thing that makes me the most upset is the simple fact that they didn't even have the decency to acknowledge the fact that they received your message or to even call and tell you that they were sorry to hear about your grandmother death".

My mom then continued eating her breakfast. But I could tell that she was extremely angry about the whole situation. When I replied "Well I guess so", I was giving Suzanne and Robert the benefit of a doubt simply because I was taking into consideration the fact that I had explained to them that Mitchell would remember our grandmother and indeed would be hurt. But once my mom was done expressing how she felt. It hit me that I felt the exact same way. Suzanne and Robert could have at least had the decency to call and at least say that they were sorry to hear about what had happened. But they didn't and the thought of this now disgusted me. I then told my parents that I was done eating and that I was going to finish my make-up.

I was extremely pissed at by this time. And that's when I decided that I'd had enough. I could no longer take it anymore. Suzanne and Robert had won. They never wanted me in my brother's life to begin with. They only allowed me to come around because they knew that my brothers would be devastated if they didn't get to see me every once in awhile. But this was the final straw. I was done with it all. I'd been keeping the truth hidden from my brothers for years as well as having to endure both Suzanne and Robert phoniness for years. And I did it all for the sake of my brothers because I knew that I had no choice but to endure these things if I wanted to be apart of their lives, but not anymore. I vowed at this point to myself that I wouldn't do it anymore. And as hard as it is for me to say, from that day on I felt as if I no longer had two younger brothers named Mitchell and Jacob.

I'm human just like everyone else. I can only endure so much pain and hurt. And at this point of time, it no longer hurt when I said, "Mitchell and Jacob are no longer my brothers". I hope that one day both of my brothers as well as the many other people that have asked me for many years why I don't keep in touch with my brothers can feel as well as understand were I'm coming from. I also hope that one day my brothers can understand as well as forgive me for having little involvement in both of their lives.

"Dear Mitchell and Jacob. You were the only family that I had, and now when we talk or see each other, it feels as if we're complete strangers. It's not that I didn't love you. It's just that I wasn't allowed to love you. Although I was fully aware that both of you were living happy lives that were filled with lies. I still choose to bite my tongue for years. This is something that I would normally under any circumstances ever do. But I did it for one reason and one reason only. I didn't want to hurt either one of you. And if I'm doing so now by writing this, I deeply apologize and hope that you can forgive me. The last thing that I would ever want to do is hurt either one of you in any way, shape, or form. But please try to understand that I've been hurting for years. This is something that I needed to get off my chest, as well as something that needed to be said".

Love Always,

Your one and only sister, Timesha

Chapter 23

Going Back to Illinois

My mom and I arrived at the Amtrak train station at nine thirty in the morning. My train was scheduled to leave at nine fifty-one that morning. I remember that my mom and I sat in her car as I waited for the train. I was already aware that my mom would only be able to sit with me until a quarter to ten. She had to return back home at that time so that she could baby-sit Peter and Nina because my dad was going fishing with a couple of his buddies at ten. I remember sitting next to my mom and her telling me that she felt like she was going to vomit. I knew that she was extremely nervous as well as scared for me to be returning back to Illinois. She told me that she was nervous because I would be traveling alone. She was also scared that my cousin Perry and Eboney would forget to pick me up from the train station once I arrived in Illinois. My mom also told me that in a weird way, she was scared that I wouldn't return back to Minnesota but instead stay in Illinois.

I turned to my mom and said "There's nothing for me in Illinois but bad memories. Why wouldn't I come back? Minnesota is my home now. And you guys are my family. So don't worry so much. I'll be back in three days." My mom just looked at me. And to my surprise, she didn't cry. We both got out of the car and she helped me carry my luggage over by a bench outside were I was going to wait for my train to arrive. I could have waited inside with everyone else, but it was nice outside, and plus the train would be there in five minutes. My mom then gave me a big hug and a kiss on the cheek and told me to call her once I was on the train and then she headed back home.

It was now five minutes until my train was to arrive and I was quite anxious. Well five minutes tuned into fifteen minutes, then to twenty-five minutes, and finally forty-five minutes later a woman that worked for the train station came outside and told me why their had been a delay. The woman then informed me that the reason why the train was now an hour behind scheduled was because their was a old man lying on the tracks in Minnesota City, which is ten minutes away from Winona. The woman also told me that that train didn't hit the old man. Otherwise, I was told that it would have been a three-hour delay because they would've had to wait for the corner to arrive. The woman then told me that the train would be arriving soon. And she was right. Within a matter of minutes, I saw the train from a distance coming down the tracks.

Once the train arrived, I gathered my luggage and I was the first person on the train. I was determined to be the first person on the train considering the fact that I had been standing outside in the cold for over an hour. I then called my mom and told her that I was just now leaving and told her all about the delay. She then told me to be safe and not to talk to anyone and to call her as soon as I made it to Illinois and my cousins picked me up. The train ride took five and a half hours. I brought nothing with me. No headphones to listen to music, or no magazines to read. All I had was my luggage, some snacks, and a cell phone that only had service for the first two hours of the train ride. So I slept about four of the hours away.

The time that I didn't spend sleeping, was used to use the restroom and for me to think about how awkward I returning to Illinois was going to be. However, there did come a point in time when I did meet a cute guy. He had been one of the guys that I witnesses as I was out the window smoking a cigarette outside at a rest stop. He then got back on the train and walked past me and then asked me if I had a piece of gum, and I told him "yes". I don't remember his name. But I do remember that he said that he was from Portland, SE and that he was going Springfield, IL. But this guy's cuteness soon disappeared once he told me that he had been riding the train for three days and hadn't showered. After talking to this guy, I then decided to once again go back to sleep. I decided that I'd wake up once we arrived in Milwaukee, WI because then Chicago would be the next stop after that.

I must admit that throughout the entire train ride I wasn't nervous at all. The moment that I became nervous was at four thirty in the afternoon, when I arrived in Chicago, and then stepped off the train. I remember that it was then that my heart began to beat extremely fast. I became very hot, and then began to breathe very heavily. I also remember that my legs became very weak, and that there even came a point in time when I felt like I was going to faint. But then I quickly pulled myself together. I then began looking around to try and see if I saw anyone that remotely resembled what my cousin Perry and Eboney had looked like seven years ago. I had no luck. I then realized that we were just kid's back then that hadn't even gone through puberty yet. Not to mention the fact that I probably wouldn't be able to tell the difference between them and a complete stranger. I then called my cousin Perry's cell phone. Grandma Yolanda had giving his number once he had agreed to pick me up.

Perry answered the phone, just as I knew he would. I had spoken with him earlier and explained to him that I had a delay and that I would be an hour behind schedule. He told me that was fine and that they would still get there at the time that we planned just so that they would be there no matter when I arrived. Perry answered the phone and I told him that I was there and asked him where he was. He then told me that he was parked outside and that he would send Eboney to look for me. I then told him that I was in the process of trying to find my way out of the train station and that I would call him back once I was outside.

Once I was out side I noticed that it was complete chaos. There were so many cars, so many people, and so much traffic. This was something that I hadn't seen in years, and it fascinated me. I called then Perry back and told him the name of the street that I was on. He then told me that he was going to give Eboney his phone so that I could talk to her and tell her where I was so that we could meet up with each other. Eboney and I talked for almost three minutes. We then realized that we were at the opposite end of the train station from each other. I told her the name of a street that I was near and she told me that she was near that street as well. She then told me to just keep walking straight and that we would eventually meet up with each other. By now five minutes had passed by. And then I came face to face with Eboney, my cousin that I hadn't seen in seven years.

"Oh my God! You look just like your mama", were the first words out of my mouth once I saw Eboney. We then gave each other a great big hug, and I stood there with tears running down my face. She then helped me carry my luggage up the street a little more too where Perry's car was parked. To my surprise, Eboney still looked the exactly same way that she did when we were younger. The only difference was that her butt was a little bit bigger, as Grandma Yolanda had told me. I then remembered back when I was younger that I was always jealous of Eboney, because she had longer hair and bigger boobs than I did. But that jealousy was no longer there. We were both grown up now, and the only feelings that I had for her were feeling of joy. I had feelings of joy, because I hadn't seen her in seven years. I knew that we had a lot of catching up to do.

Once we were at Perry's car, I noticed that he was in his in the trunk of his car moving his speakers around so that I would have room for my luggage. And my heart began to beat even faster. Perry then came up from behind the trunk with a smile on his face, and gave me a hug, and more tears rolled down my face. Once again, to my surprise, Perry still looked exactly the same as she had when we were younger. The only difference was that Perry was very, very, tall, with a deep voice and slight mustache. Other than that, he was still my little cousin that I used to bet up all the time when I was younger. But now I wouldn't even think about trying to pick a fight with him. Because this time, I know that I'd lose.

Once I was all suddled in, my cousins told me that they didn't know when Chantel was, and then asked me if I wanted to visit their younger sister Chevonne, and I told them "Yes". The last time that I had seen Chevonne, was in January of 1997 and she was only five years old. I was fully aware that she was now thirteen simply because she's nine days younger than my brother Mitchell. So needless to say, Chevonne was the person that I was most excited to see. I think that this was mainly because I had seen how much Mitchell had matured over the years and I was sure that she had done the same. I think that another major reason why I was so excited to see Chevonne, was because I had watched both her and Mitchell grow from being babies to little five year olds in pre-school.

Eboney and I talked to each other, as Perry drove us to his house in Chicago so that I could see Chevonne as well as meet their foster parents. Perry and Chevonne had been living in a foster home with a woman by the name of Rebecca since the summer of 1997, due to the stroke that Grandma Yolanda suffered from the year before. Eboney and I talked among each other and I found out that she was twenty-one years old with three kids. I also found out that her older sister Chantel, who's twenty-four, had a seven year old son. I'd heard that Chantel also had two other children, but one died shortly after birth and the other was living with the grandparents on the father's side of the family. I also found out that neither Perry, Eboney, Chantel, nor Chevonne are allowed to keep in contact with their other two younger siblings who were being cared for by another adoptive family.

Once I arrived to Perry and Chevonne's house, I was greeted by several little kids. Perry had told me that Rebecca had a lot of foster kids. But out of all the kids that I was surrounded by, I knew exactly which one was my cousin. I say Chevonne sitting in of the television with a big puffy ponytail on the left side of her head. I was then introduced to Rebecca who offered me a seat right away. She seemed like a very nice woman. She even told me that she had just taken in a little boy that was from Minnesota, but she couldn't remember which city he was from. I was at that point that Chevonne took her attention off the television and began to focus on me. She looked me up and down. And I did the same to her. It was at that point that Rebecca said "Chevonne you better get up and give your cousin a hug"! And Chevonne did.

I was extremely happy that Rebecca said something other wise I don't know how long we would have continued staring at each other. The hug had broken the silence and Chevonne and I began to talk to each other. She was mostly concerned about Mitchell and she told me that they had spoken to each on the phone while she was visiting Grandma Yolanda in the summer of 2004. Overall, I enjoyed talking to Chevonne very much. But I must admit that even though she was only thirteen, I extremely awkward around her. I believe that this was mainly because I didn't know what to say to her. Perry, Eboney, I had all grown up together and had many things to reminisce about. But this was something that I kept searching for with Chevonne, but never found.

After Chevonne and I were done getting reacquainted with each other, it was time for Perry to drop me off at Grandma Yolanda's house. Grandma Yolanda's is where I would be staying until I was to return back to Minnesota. I said, "nice meeting you" and "good-bye" to everyone, and off Perry, Eboney, and I went. As were driving to Grandma Yolanda's house in Maywood, Perry's phone rang. It was the father of Eboney's children Ted on the other line and he wanted to know if Perry would come and pick him up. Perry agreed to pick him up and told him that we'd be there shortly. By now it was around six thirty in the evening and extremely dark. And I must admit that I was a little scared to be driving around on the south side of Chicago.

I noticed that there were a lot of people standing outside on a corner by a bus stop. That's when Eboney told Perry to drive towards them because that's where Ted was standing. As soon as Perry pulled over by all of the people who were standing on the corner, many of those people immediately began to swarm around the car in order to try and see who was inside. It was then that Eboney replied, "There go Chantel right there"! I looked out the window and sure enough, it was my cousin Chantel. She was one of the many people standing on the corner.

Perry put his car into park, as Chantel yelled over at him to wait because she needed to talk to him. Within a matter of seconds, Chantel appeared on the passenger side of Perry's car and started talking to him about her maybe coming out to Grandma Yolanda's house later. I was sitting in the back seat of the car when she looked in and replied "Perry, who's that girl in your back seat"? And he replied, "That's Timesha, I told you that I was going to pick her up tonight"! Chantel then replied "Hell naw! Ya'll better let my lil' cousin up out this car"! Chantel then began to scream due to the fact that she was so happy to see me.

I then proudly got out of the back seat of Perry's car with a big smile on my face. I walked over by Chantel and she by far gave me the tightest as well as longest hug that I have ever received in my life. After Chantel and I were done hugging each other, we then pulled away from each other and began to talk about what was going on in our lives. It was then that I noticed that Chantel was extremely skinny, for having giving birth to three kids. Then asked her what size she was and she replied, "Girl, I were a size three. And half of the time I can't even fit into them". I then replied, "Man I wear a size five and everybody tells me that I'm skinny. But compared too you I probably look like a heavyweight". And we both laughed.

I would guess that Chantel and I probably stood on the corner and talked to each other for at least a half an hour. Also, within this half an hour, I also caught on to the fact that Chantel was a little bit tipsy. I picked up on this simply by the way she was acting, and I also smelled beer on her breath. Later, towards the end of our conversation, Chantel would admit to drinking a 40oz before she had came outside that night and that she was going to drink some more once we left to go to Grandma Yolanda's house. It was at this point that I realized how much drinking truly ran in my family genes. I would later hear from Egg that Chantel had also tried experimenting with crack cocaine as well. But who's to say if Egg was even telling the truth.

I'm assuming that Perry got tired of waiting and then he asked "Chantel are you coming out to Grandma's house with us or not"? Chantel then replied "Naw, I gonna catch a ride out there later". So that was it. Eboney, Ted, and I hopped back into Perry's car and off we went to Grandma Yolanda's house. Once we arrived to Grandma Yolanda's house, Eboney rang the buzzer and Grandma Yolanda buzzed us in. All four of us then walked up stairs to Grandma Yolanda's apartment. Once we were inside I gave her a great big hug. Grandma Yolanda was the only family member that had kept in contact with me since I'd left Illinois, and although I had seen her in the summer of 2003 at my graduation party, it felt as if I hadn't seen her in seven years as well.

Grandma Yolanda, Perry, Eboney, Ted, Shelly (my cousin & also Auntie Lola's daughter), June (Grandma Yolanda's long time friend), and I spent at least an hour in a half talking to each other. I remembered both Shelly and June. They both had known me since I was a little baby and were extremely happy to see me. Most of the time that the seven of us spent together was spent talking about the good old days. Grandma Yolanda had a ton of pictures hanging up around her house. Most of these pictures were of my brothers and I. But I figured that this was simply because Grandma Yolanda was the only family member who had kept in contact with us, which would mean that she was the only one that would have pictures of us. My cousins and I enjoyed these pictures very much. We spent a lot of time making fun of how silly my cousins and I looked when we were younger.

Although we were all having a grand old time, there did come a time where a slight argument broke out. This was due to the fact that Grandma Mrs. Rolland had passed away three days ago, and no one had any idea as to when her funeral was going to be. Grandma Yolanda told us that she didn't know anything about when or where the funeral was going to be because Otis, Wes, and one of Auntie Ellen's friends were taken care of it and told her that the didn't need her help. I then said "Let me get this straight, we're talking about your mother here and they're telling you that they don't need your help. Then why is it that they have some women who isn't even apart of our family helping"? It was at this point that my cousins and I became extremely upset. I then asked Grandma Yolanda for Auntie Ellen's phone number. I told her that I wanted to talk to Otis. Grandma Yolanda then became extremely upset as well and declined to give me the number. It was at this point that I saw how upset the topic made her and I decided to drop it. At least for that night anyways. It would only be a matter of time before I found out the real reason why Otis, Wes, and Auntie Ellen's friend Grace didn't want Grandma Yolanda's help.

It was around nine o'clock at night when everyone decided to call it a night. Grandma Yolanda's apartment was completely cleared out. It was just her and I. We then decided that we would call it a night as well. Grandma Yolanda had a spare bedroom in her apartment and that was where I was going to sleep. So we put our pajamas on and the both of us laid in her bed and we watched television for awhile. But the night wouldn't end there; I still had more family members that were stopping by to see me. The first one to stop by was my older cousin Tommy who is five years my senior. Tommy stopped by with his wife Debra and his two-year-old daughter Jessica. It was kind of funny because I noticed that

Jessica was staring at me funny for a long time. She then walked over to her mother and asked her "Mama is that Timesha"? Her mother replied, "Yes" and then told me that Jessica knew who I was due to the numerous pictures that Grandma Yolanda had lying around the house and that Jessica was always asked about me.

Tommy and his family didn't stay long, and once they left my cousin Mario, whom I believe is thirteen years my senior stopped by. Mario is Shelly's youngest son and he had heard that I was in town and wanted to see me. Next I would receive a phone call from my Auntie Lola. Auntie Lola is the mother of Shelly and the grandmother of Mario. The four of us are related to each other through marriage. These are also three people that have known me since the day I was born. If I'm not mistaking, I'm pretty sure that Auntie Lola was my great-grandfather Ernest James Rolland Sr.'s sister. After I was done talking to Auntie Lola, I received a phone call from my cousin Nichelle. Nichelle is Tommy's older sister, and she had also heard that I was in town and wanted to talk to me and she told me that she would be stopping by to see me before I headed back to Minnesota.

But out of all the visits and phone calls that I received that night, the last phone call was by far the most important. The last phone call came from Uncle Ike. Uncle Ike was Grandma Yolanda's oldest child. This call was the most important simply because it dealt with Grandma Mrs. Rolland's funeral arrangements. It was doing this conversation that Uncle Ike informed me that Wes had told him that the funeral probably wasn't going to be until Thursday or Friday. And my heart dropped. I shouted, "It can't be on Thursday or Friday! I'm leaving to go back to Minnesota at two o'clock in the afternoon on Wednesday"! Before getting off the phone with Uncle Ike, he told me not to say anything to anyone about what he had just told me simply because it wasn't a for sure thing. And I agreed.

But I had already made up my mind. As far as I was concerned it was a for sure thing. It was at that point that I became extremely angry and decided that I should call it a night. I laid down that night with one thing on my mind and one thing only. And that was Grandma Mrs. Rolland's funeral. As I laid in the dark for hours, I made up my mind that night that

I was going to somehow find out Auntie Ellen's phone number. I needed answers. I needed to hear first hand what was being done about my Grandma Mrs. Rolland's funeral arranges. I knew that Grandma Yolanda was the only one that had the number. My mission for the next day was to find someone else who had the number as well.

Chapter 24

Some Things Are Better Left Unknown

It was now Monday December 6, 2004. The first thing that I did that morning when I woke up was called me cousin Perry. I had noticed that the night before when Eboney and I were shouting that we wanted Auntie Ellen's phone number, that he was extremely quiet. This led me to believe that he himself had the number or that he knew of someone else who did. To my surprise I was right. Perry indeed had the number but he told me that he just didn't want to say anything about it that night. He also told me not to tell anyone who I got the number from, and I agreed. My mission was now complete. I had the number and now I could finally get some answers. So I thought.

I called Auntie Ellen's and Otis answered the phone. I explained to him who I was and why I was calling. I told him that "I just got into town last night and I'm only here until Wednesday afternoon. Do you know if the funeral is going to be before then"? Otis then told me that he really wasn't sure because he wasn't planning it. He informed me that Wes and Grace were planning the funeral and that by the sound of things that Thursday was the earliest that the funeral would be. I then told him that "It'd be really nice if the funeral was on Wednesday or even Thursday, because I'm sure that I could get my train ticketed pushed back another day". I then asked Otis for Wes phone number and he gave it to me.

So my mission wasn't complete after all. Otis had only told me information that I already knew. But Wes was the person that I need to talk too. I called Wes's house and his wife Wanda answered the phone. She told me that Wes was at work. She also told me what time he got off of work and that I should call him back then. We talked for awhile and I remember saying to her "The only reason for me coming back to Illinois was to say my final good-byes to my grandmother and to see her be put to rest and I would be extremely hurt if I wasn't able to do so". Wanda then told me that she totally agreed with me. But once again she didn't know what was going on, because Wes and Grace were in charge.

I then got off the phone with Wanda and called my mom. I complained to her about how unorganized my family was and that the funeral wasn't going to be until Thursday at the earliest. She then asked me if I wanted to stay an extra day and I told her yes. She told me that that would be fine. Next I called down to the Amtrak train station to try and find out if they could switch my ticket from Wednesday until Thursday and they told me that that wouldn't be a problem. I then got up and told Grandma Yolanda that I would be staying an extra day. When she asked why, I told her that I had spoken to Otis and what he had told me about the funeral situation. I also told her that I had called Wes's house and spoken with Wanda and that I would be calling him again once he got off work. Grandma Yolanda was listening to everything that I was saying, but at the same time she was rolling her eyes.

I became a little annoyed and asked her "Why are you acting like this? Why are you so mad at them?" And to this day, this was a question that I wished that I hadn't asked. Because what I learned has filled my heart with hate that I never knew existed. Hate that no matter how hard anyone tries and no matter what anyone says to try and make me think different will ever be erased. I sat on the corner of my grandma's bed as she told me the real reason why Otis, Wes, and Grace didn't want her help in planning her own mother's funeral. I sat next to my grandmother with tears in my eyes and hate in my heart as she spoke to me.

I really can't go too much into details for obvious reasons, but we'll just say that it all started back in 1998 when Grandma Mrs. Rolland was sent to live in a nursing home. Grandma Mrs. Rolland had stated to lose her memory and everyone agreed that she shouldn't be left alone. Grandma Mrs. Rolland was sent to live in a nice nursing home that was located in Oak Park, IL. It was at this point that SOMEONE became her power of atterntoy. This meant that SOMEONE was the only person that was in charge of everything that had to deal with Grandma Mrs. Rolland, including her money.

But as we all know, there's only so many shopping sprees, fur coats, trips to Las Vegas, and Hotel parties that you can have before you start to run out of money! And once the funds ran low, Grandma Mrs. Rolland was then taken out of her upscale nursing home and moved into a cheaper one. It had even gone so far as SOMEONE forgetting to pay Grandma Mrs. Rolland's monthly storage fee. This meant that all of Grandma Mrs. Rolland's belongings were now sitting outside of the storage. But it would only be a matter of time before all of SOMEONE's wrong doings would catch up to her. In 2002 SOMEONE came face to face with karma. This is the year that SOMEONE would suffer for all the bad things that she had been doing. This is the year that SOMEONE would suffer from a stroke and no longer be able to talk or walk anymore. The old saying what goes around comes around, is the perfect example in this case.

After hearing all of this information from Grandma Yolanda, I sat in disbelief. It all made sense to me why Otis, Wes, and Grace were all acting shady towards her. It was at that point that I realized why Grandma Yolanda wasn't allowed to take part in the planning of her mother's funeral. It was also at that point why I realized why she became so angry the night before when we were talking about the funeral arrangements. But it was also at this point that I became very upset about how much my great grandmother was taken advantage of by her own flesh and blood.

It's one thing to be taking advantage of by a complete stranger, but when it comes to being taken advantage of by your own blood, that's just something that one can't even put into words. Grandma Mrs. Rolland had become very sick, as she grew older. She needed some one to look after her and the one person who she thought would be fit for the job betrayed her. Grandma Mrs. Rolland was practically on her death bed. And SOMEONE saw this as a free ride to do what they wanted to do with her money. Because after all, Grandma Mrs. Rolland had lost her memory and wouldn't remember anyway.

This is one of the lowest and sickest things that could've been done. I believed every word that Grandma Yolanda told me, not to mention the fact that four other family members would later verify it. And now, this gave me all the more reason to want to talk to Wes. I called Wes's house that very same day, but no one answered. I called again the next day, and still no answer. I called Auntie Ellen's house as well, no answer. To this day, no one ever answered the phone for me. This gave me all the more reason to believe that Grandma Yolanda was indeed telling the truth.

After Grandma Yolanda and I were done talking, we then walked over to a store that was near by. Grandma Yolanda needed to buy a container of hair gel as well as a pack of cigarettes. Once we were done at the store I told her that I was going for a walk and that I would be back shortly and she told me that was fine as long as I made it back before it got dark. "Timesha, Maywood isn't like it was seven years ago. You're unlike anything that these guys have seen before. So make sure you get back here before it gets dark" are the words that my grandma said to me as I headed out the door. I already knew where I was going. I was going to walk from Maywood to Brodview. This is a walk that took me a little bit over a half an hour, but it was a walk that I had to make. It had been seven years and now I was coming face to face with my past.

My first stop was Roosevelt Elementary. This was the grade school that I had attended for six years. The sight of this orange and black school made me smile. I thought back to when I was a little girl and how I used to love jumping rope outside of the school. I also remembered playing at the park and I even remembered how Perry and I used to always race each other home from school, and I'd win nine times out of ten. I arrived to the school around four in the afternoon and the school was actually close. However there was a little girl standing by the doorway and she let me in. the first thing that I did once I was inside of the school was walked over to the wall where they used to hang the pictures of the eight grade graduating students. I then looked at the class of 1999 of whom I would have graduated with and I only knew seven out of at least thirty people.

I then slowly walked down the hallway that I ran down everyday when I was younger. I then walked into the school office that was set up exactly as it had been seven years earlier and said "Hi, my name is Timesha Mohan and I used to go to school here when I was younger. I'm in town visiting and I was just wondering if you could tell me if any of my old teachers still teach here"? I then proceeded to give all the names of my teachers starting with kindergarten and stopping at sixth grade. Technically I wasn't in sixth grade because Egg had tried having me held back. But I was in Mr. Pearson's class and he taught both fifth and sixth grade and he let me do sixth grade work. However, only 1 out of the seven teachers still taught there. And that was Ms. Keeves.

Ms. Reeves was my third grade teacher that taught me a great lesson early on in life. That lesson was that I couldn't trust anyone as well as to keep my mouth shut. But it was now ten years later and I had healed from the "pull you pants down and lay over these two chairs with your bare Ass in the air" beating. I no longer had hard harsh feeling towards her anymore. I just simply wanted to let her know that I was telling the truth ten years ago. But most of all I wanted to let her know that I was no longer living with Egg and that I was doing much better now. But I never got to see or talk to Ms. Keeves because by the time I got to the school, she was already left for the day.

After I left the school I went to go and visit the old apartment building that I had lived in for six years. This apartment building was a block away from the school; so it didn't take me long to get there. I stood in front of the very same white apartment building were most of my childhood years took place. My knees buckled as I stood in front of the building with tears in my eyes. I wanted so desperately to enter the building and knock on the door to Grandma Mrs. Rolland's old apartment. But I couldn't due to the fact that there was now a big black metal gate with spikes at the top of it keeping away from the building. This is a gate that wasn't there seven years ago. I stood there as if I was frozen staring at the lock on the gate wishing that I had a key to unlock it and get inside. I also stared at the six doorbells that I couldn't ring because the gate guarded them as well.

I stood in front of my old apartment building trying to think of a way that I could get inside of the gate. After about five minutes or so it became very clear to me that there wasn't a way that I could get inside of the gate. I then turned around and proceeded to head back to Grandma Yolanda's house. As I walked down the street I looked at the house that was located across the alley from the apartment building that I used to live in and smiled. I smiled simply because I remembered that seven years ago Grandma Mrs. Rolland used to baby-sit a little boy by the name of Keith that lived there. I remembered that my Keith and I used to play together when we were younger and that he had the biggest crush on me. I then said to myself "I wonder if Keith still lives there". I then decided that since I couldn't get into my old apartment building and had nothing else to do, that I would go and find out.

I then walked up to the door, and I must admit that my heart was beating extremely fast when I knocked on the door. I remembered thinking "What if Keith doesn't live there anymore, I'm going to look so stupid"! Or worst "What if Keith does still live there and he doesn't remember who I am"! But I knocked anyway. Within a matter of seconds a not so little boy without a shirt on peaked out of the front window. I was sure that it was Keith. The boy then came and opened the down with a confused look on his face and said "Hey". But before he could say anything else I took over the conversation by saying "I don't know if you remember me or not, but my name is Timesha and I used to live in the apartment right behind you. We used to hang out when we were younger and my Grandma Mrs. Rolland used to baby sit you"!

Keith then looked at me again, and then a big smile came across his face and then Keith replied "Oh yeah I remember you! Come in, come in"! Once I was inside Keith told me to have a seat. I then walked over and sat down on the couch while Keith sat in a chair. I then learned that this little boy wasn't a little boy anymore and that he would be turning eighteen in just two months. As Keith and I talked to each other I noticed that he kept staring and smiling at me throughout our entire conversation. Keith would later tell me that the reason why he kept staring and smiling at me was because he had remembered me as a little girl and that he was comparing what I looked like then to what I looked like now. Keith told me "You look exactly the same as you did when you were little. The only difference is that you just matured. But in a good way"! I then told Keith that he looked the same as well.

As time passed by Keith asked me if I had moved back to Broadview. I told him no and that the only reason why I was back was because Grandma Mrs. Rolland had passed away. And then once I heard the words come out of my mouth, I started to cry. Keith then told me that he was sorry to hear of her passing away and that he knew exactly what I was going through because his grandfather, of whom he was raised by, had just passed away as well. We then began to talk about silly things that we did when we were younger. We talked about how we used to always eat Ramen noodles together after everyday after school as well as him having a crush on me. Talking with Keith also triggered more memories about my grandmother. Keith remembered that when we were younger and came home after school that Grandma Mrs. Rolland, who had bad knees used to always throw the keys to the apartment out of the window and we'd run to catch it so that we could get into the building.

But our time spent together soon came to an end when my phone rang. It was Grandma Yolanda; she was calling to tell me to hurry home because it was getting dark. I then told Keith that it was nice seeing him and that I had to go. I did however get his phone number told him that I would call him later that night. I must admit that I was extremely happy as I walked back to Grandma Yolanda's house. I was happy that I had chosen to knock on Keith's door simply because he was a reminder of my past. Keith helped trigger my memory of things that I'm more than certain that I wouldn't have remembered. But I must admit that I was extremely amazed of how handsome Keith had turned out to be. I then remembered back when we were younger and he liked me and I could've cared less. I was a tomboy then and the last thing on my mind was a boy. The only boy that I had ever really liked was Dustin, and once he rejected me I was done with boys.

As I walked back to Grandma Yolanda's house it had began to get dark, and I must admit that I became a little scared. I then called Nichole and she agreed to talk to me until I got to my grandma's house. While talking to Nichole about my day, I all of a sudden shouted, "Damn it". Nichole then asked me what was wrong and that's when I told her that I was so amazed with everything that was going around me when I was in Broadview that I for got to take my camera out of my purse and take pictures of my old house or school for my scrap book. Once I arrived back at Grandma Yolanda's house she informed me that my Uncle John had called. Uncle John was Sperm's older brother. She told me that she had told him that I would be coming into town and that he wanted to see me. She also told me that Egg would be arriving in Chicago at nine o'clock that night. She also told me that Tommy would be taking me down to the Greyhound bus station to pick her up. I really didn't want to go with him to pick her up, but I knew that I was the one and person that knew what she looked like after seven years. So I agreed to go with him.

It was about a quarter to nine when Tommy, Jessica, and I went to the Greyhound bus station to pick up Egg. When we arrived at the train station Tommy told me that he would wait out front in the car with Jessica, while I went inside to try and find Egg. I walked inside the train station a looked around a couple of times but I didn't see Egg. I then walked outside and told Tommy that I couldn't find Egg. I then told him that I was going back inside to look for her again and that I would also ask the person at the desk if the bus from Minnesota had come in yet. Once I was back inside of the bus station I asked the woman at the front desk if the bus from Minnesota had come in yet and she told me yes and that it had came in fifteen minutes ago. I then looked around again for Egg and that's when I spotted her. She was standing in the middle of a huge group of people in a blue sweatshirt with three big duffle bags.

I then approached Egg and of course she had to give me a hug and one of her famous "I miss you so much" speeches. This was the first time that Egg and I had seen each other since my graduation back in June 2003. I then told her that she should have waited outside for us and to hurry up because Tommy had been illegally parked out front for over twenty minutes. Egg and I then walked outside to Tommy's car, where he then popped his trunk and put Egg's duffle bags inside. Tommy then drove us back to Grandma Yolanda's house. We arrived back at Grandma Yolanda's house around ten in the evening. The first words out of Egg mouth once we were inside the house were "Timesha, let me borrow a couple of dollars from you so I can run the street and get some chicken from Popeyes". I then told her "I'm giving you three dollars and three dollars only! I need to eat too"!

It was within a matter of minutes when Egg decided that she didn't want chicken anymore, instead she wanted tacos. So Egg, being the inconsiderate person that she is, didn't even take into consideration that Tommy had to work the following morning. Instead she begged him into driving ten minutes away to a restaurant so that she could have tacos. They arrived back at the house within a half an hour. Egg walked through the door with two tacos and a bowl of ice cream from Baskin Robins. I then asked Egg how much the tacos were and she told me a dollar and forty something cents each. This led me to believe one of two things. One, which Egg had her own money and just, wanted to see how more money she could get off me. Or two, Egg had begged Tommy into buying tacos or ice cream for her. I decided that both one and two would have been extremely low of her. I didn't care what she had done because I knew that she wouldn't be getting another dime from me. I then decide to call it a night. I let Egg sleep in the spare bedroom and I slept in the living room.

Chapter 25
Memories of the Past

Tuesday, December 7, 2004 was the day that I decided that I would be returning back to Minnesota on Wednesday instead of Thursday. I was fully aware that my grandmother's funeral wasn't going to be until Friday. So why should I stick around until Thursday? The only think that sticking around to Thursday would do is piss me off even more because I'd know that I wouldn't be able to attend my grandmother's funeral the following day. I awoke that morning to Grandma Yolanda telling me that I had a phone call. I was Auntie Lola. She had called to tell me that she wanted me to come out to her house and see her before I went back to Minnesota. She also told me that she would back for my car far there and back. So I agreed, I told her that I had to get dressed and that I would call her back.

While I was getting dressed I received another phone call. It was Uncle John. He had called to tell me that he and Sperm wanted to see me as well and that he would send my Uncle Dollar to pick me up. Uncle Dollar's real name was Quincy. I had known him all my entire life. He and Sperm had grown up together, and this is how Grandpa Berry met his second wife Beth, because Beth was Uncle Dollar's mother. Also Uncle Dollar was the person that introduced Egg to Eric (Mitchell's dad). And the name Uncle Dollar is what I used to call him when I was younger. I called him this simply because when I was a little girl he would give me a dollar every time I saw him.

I then told Uncle John that I would come out to Chicago later on that evening because I was going to be spending that afternoon with my aunt. Uncle John said that was fine and for me to call him whenever I was ready for Uncle Dollar to come and pick me up. After I got off the phone with Uncle John, I then went back to getting ready. I then noticed that Egg wasn't in the spare bedroom. I asked Grandma Yolanda where she was and she told me that she had gone upstairs to visit Shelly. I had just gotten done getting ready when Egg ventured back downstairs. She asked me where I was going and I told her "Right now, I'm going over to Lola's house. And later on I'm going to hang out with The Mullins"! Egg then told me to come upstairs to Shelly's apartment because Matt was there and he wanted to see me. Matt was Shelly's oldest son and he was also my live in baby sitter while Egg and I lived in Forest Park, IL. I knew that Matt was my cousin, but I still always called him Uncle Matt when I was younger. I was very fond of him when I was younger, so I was excited to see him. It had been well over twelve years sense we had last seen each other.

Once I arrived to Shelly's apartment I was surprised to see Matt. He had looked exactly the same as he did the last time that I had seen him. As for me, he said that he was surprised to see how grown up I was now, because I couldn't have been more than seven years old the last time that he saw me. We then talked for awhile and then I told him that had to go because I was going to visit his grandmother. He then told me to call Lola and tell her that she didn't have to call a cab because he would bring me over to her house. Matt spent a little more time talking and then he asked me if I was ready to go and I told him yes. And as you could've guessed that Egg invited herself to come and visit Auntie Lola as well.

Uncle Matt decided that he was going to stop by the liquor store on the way to Lola's house. Before he went into the store he asked Egg if she wanted anything and she told him yes and that she would go inside with him. He asked me if I wanted anything as well and I told him "No, Thanks", and he and Egg headed into the store. Within a matter of minutes, Egg walked out of the store and over to the car and asked me if I wanted anything to drink. And once again I replied "No". Egg then said, "Come on Baby Girl we've never drank together before". And once again a declined by saying, "No thanks, I'm really not in the drinking mood". Which was true, I really wasn't in the drinking mood. But most of all, it was because I didn't want to get drunk with Egg. Plus in my eyes only people who don't have lives or people who are alcoholics drink at one in the afternoon.

Egg and I must have stayed at Lola's house for at least three hours. Within these three hours, every time that I'd leave the room I'd hear Egg whining to Lola about how she knows that she screwed up and how much she loves my brothers and I. During this visit I also got to spent time with Lola's youngest daughter Angel. I believe that Angel was one year older than my cousin Mario. So, that would make here at least thirteen or fourteen years my senior. I always envied Angel when I was younger simple because she was a tall and skinny beautiful girl that was in college. She also had her own car, and when I was younger I always said that I wanted to look like her when I was older. It had been at least eight or nine years sense I had last seen her. But she was still as beautiful as she was when I was younger. But this time around, it was a little different. Angel was now the one telling me how beautiful I was. Also within these three hours I stuffed my stomach full on homemade catfish with hot sauce. This is a dish that I hadn't eaten since I'd moved to Minnesota.

But of course my visit with Auntie Lola wouldn't end without her trying to make me feel sorry for Egg and trying to make me believe in God. Lola was trying her best to get me to tell Egg that I loved her. But that was something that I just couldn't see myself doing. The fact of the matter was that I wasn't even sure if I loved Egg or not. And if I did have any love for Egg at all it was simply due to the fact that she gave birth to me. Now me saying that I don't love Egg doesn't mean that I hate her either. I don't hate anyone; I just hate Egg's ways.

Now when the topic of God came up, that was something that I really didn't want to talk about at all. I simple told Auntie Lola "How can I believe in something when I have no proof that it actually exist. And if there is a God, he's never answered one of my preys." Lola then asked me "What have you preyed for that God didn't answer". I then told her "When I was a little girl I used to always prey for a better life". And she replied "It looks like your living a better life now". "Sure I am, but that has absolutely nothing to do with God. It has to do with my mom selling drugs to the cops and getting caught"! I shouted. And that was the end of our conversation. I could tell that I had hurt Auntie Lola's feeling, but I didn't care. I didn't love Egg and didn't believe in God, and no matter how hard she tried, she wasn't going to make me think anything different.

After I was done spending time with Auntie Lola, it was now time for me to go and visit The Mullins. So I called up Uncle Dollar and told him that I was now ready for him to come and pick me up from Lola's house. While I was talking to him on the phone I also spoke to Sperm. Sperm and I had been talking for a couple of minutes when Egg walked into the room. She asked me who I was talking to and I told her. She then asked if she could speak with him. I told Sperm that Egg wanted to talk to him and then I gave her the phone. But after the phone was already in her hand, I wished I hadn't given it to her. The first words out of her mouth were "Kevin we'll get there when we get there. You've had nineteen years to be involved in her life......"! And that's when I snatched the phone out of her hand and replied "That wasn't even necessary"! I then apologized to Sperm for Egg's rude behavior and told him that I would see him shortly.

After I got off the phone with Sperm I thought about what Egg had said "We'll get there when we get there". No one had even invited Egg to come with, but once again she invited herself. I must admit that I was a little upset that Egg was going to be tagging along simply because I hadn't seen Sperm in seven years and it was quite obvious that she was going to continue to keep meddling with other people's business. But I decided that I'd make the best of it and pretend like Egg wasn't even there. I was about an hour and a half later when Uncle Dollar arrived. He walked into Auntie Lola's house and gave everyone a hug. I asked him what took him so long, and he replied that he had gotten lost. I noticed shortly after talking go him that he smelled a lot like alcohol. I asked him if he had been drinking and he told me that he had had a couple of beers. I asked him if he needed me to drive but he said that he was fine to drive.

So Egg and I hopped into the car with him and off we went. We arrived at my Aunt Donna's house within fifteen minutes. Donna is the younger sister of Grandpa Berry. As Uncle Dollar, Egg, and I approached the house there was a girl standing in the doorway giving us a mean look. Uncle Dollar went up to the door and opened it. The girl replied, "Who are you looking for"? Uncle Dollar replied, "The Mullins, isn't this their house"? The girl replied "No! They live next door". It was at thin point that both Egg and I started to laugh. Uncle Dollar had taken us to the wrong house. Sure enough the girl was right when she said that The Mullins lived next door, because as soon as I walked over to the next house I saw Sperm standing in the doorway. He looked exactly the same way that he had looked seven years ago when I left for Minnesota. As soon as I walked inside the doorway Sperm gave me a big hug and we walked upstairs. Once upstairs I was reintroduced to Uncle John, Aunt Donna, her husband Uncle Jerry, their son Zack, one of Sperm's long time friend's Bill, and my cousin Tasha.

Sperm and I then sat down at the dining room table and talked to each other. I didn't know where Egg had gone to but I was glad that she wasn't near me. This way I could have a little alone time with Sperm. Sperm and I talked a little more and then he pointed out a picture of my Uncle Donald that my cousin Tasha was were on her t-shirt. And I broke down. It was a picture of Uncle Donald throwing up the peace sign with one of the biggest smiles that I had ever seen on anyone's face. And I cried. I cried because he looked so happy in the picture and now he was gone. It was around that time that Egg entered the dining room from the kitchen and attempted to comfort me. But I told her that I was fine. I didn't need her pity and I sure as hell didn't need her of all people to comfort me.

After I was calm again I found out that the only reason why Egg had came into the dining room was to see if I wanted to go into the kitchen and drink with her and The Mullins. It was at this point that Uncle John came and joined Sperm and I. I asked them what had happen to Donald. I really can't go too much into details for obvious reasons, but we'll just say that Uncle Donald was at the wrong place at the wrong time. I guess the police received a call about a stolen car that fit the description of the vehicle that Uncle Donald was driving. To sum up the story, Uncle Donald was shot and killed by a Chicago police office. According to Sperm, Donald went down from the first shot but his foot stayed on the gas paddle and this is what caused the officer to fire off additional rounds.

171

Sperm also told me that Grandpa Berry was in the process of filing a wrongful death suit against the Chicago Police Department and the he even had Johnny

Sperm told me that if Grandpa Barry won the case that he would be looking a receiving a couple of million dollars. He then replied, "You know that your Granddad doesn't need any money. But he has to do it because it's our only way of getting some kind of justice for Donald". Sperm also told me that Donald's death hurt him a lot because he was in jail for at the time when it happened. Sperm stated "I'll never forget that I was in jail and at first I wasn't even going to go to his funeral because I didn't want my family to see me like that as well as to be in cuffs when I said good-bye to my little brother. But I went anyway because I know that I wouldn't have gone that I never would've forgiven myself. I remember that I was escorted in hand and foot cuffs by several police officers. Before I was allowed to go into the funeral home everyone else had to be cleared out of the funeral home. I remember that a couple of the police officers told me to take as long as I needed to take. I must have stood there crying for at least a half an hour. And once I was done saying good-bye to Donald, everyone else got to go back into the funeral home".

After listening to Sperm's stories I wanted to start crying all over again, but I didn't. Even though Donald had passed away five months ago, I could still see the pain in Sperm's eyes. Sperm then stated, "I'm really sorry to hear about Grandma Mrs. Rolland's death. She was a good woman. I remember years ago when she let me live with her for a month while when I was on house arrest. Do you remember that? I replied, "Yes". But the truth of the matter was that I had totally forgotten about it until he had brought it up. Sperm also told me that the reason why Grandpa Berry and Beth weren't in town was because they were in Las Vegas for a funeral and that they wouldn't be back until Thursday. "Man I know that your Granddad would sure be happy to you," stated Sperm. I replied, "I'd like to see him as well but I'm leaving for Minnesota tomorrow afternoon".

Sperm once again asked me how my brothers were doing and how old they were now. I answered his questions then asked him if he was to see a picture of then and he agreed. Sperm was surprised to see how grown up they were. Sperm then asked if Lil' Mitch and I were still as close as we had been when we were younger. Lil' Mitch is the nickname that Sperm called Mitchell. I told him that we weren't and that I talked to him and Jacob on the phone and visit with them every once in awhile. Sperm then replied "I remember that one time when I came to pick you up for one of The Mullins family reunion and you and Lil' Mitch were outside playing in the yard. I asked you if you wanted to come with and you told me that the only way you'd come with me was if Lil' Mitch could come with too. I remember that I hesitated at first. But then I saw how much your brother meant to you. And I knew that if I told you that he couldn't come with that you wouldn't have came with either. I remember that at the reunion I had people coming up to me asking me who Lil' Mitch was and told them that he was your brother and my stepson. And from that point I remembered that whenever I saw you and gave you a dollar that I gave Lil'' Mitch a dollar as well". Once again this was another memory that I remembered but had simply forgotten about until Sperm brought it up. I must admit that I was surprised with all the things that I had forgotten about, were all the things that Sperm remembered.

It was around this time that Uncle Jerry came into the dining room and asked me if I wanted a beer. I heard Egg yell from the kitchen "Jerry she ain't about to drink with you! I already tried to get her to drink with me earlier"! I told Jerry "No Thanks". And both Sperm, who was drinking and Uncle John, who wasn't drinking smiled at me. It was then that I remembered that I had a picture of me, my mom, my dad, Peter, and Nina in my wallet. I then asked Sperm and Uncle John if they wanted to see it and they said "Yes". I showed then the picture and they liked it. They said that we all looked like a happy family and that my parents looked like really nice people. Next I said "Oh yeah, I forgot to tell you that my last name isn't Mullins anymore. I legally had it changed a couple of months ago to Mohan. The last name of the family that I've been living with for the past five years". Sperm's reaction was nothing like Egg's. He simply smiled and stated, "That's fine. But you know that you'll always be Timesha Mullins to me". I must admit that I was a little surprised that he didn't ask me why I'd changed my last name from Mullins to Mohan.

It was about two and a half hours later when I left The Mullins home and headed back to Grandma Yolanda's house. But this time I remembered my camera and took pictures with Egg, Sperm, Uncle John, and Uncle Dollar. This was the first picture that I had ever had of Egg and Sperm. As well as the first picture that had ever been taken of the three of us together. Before I left Uncle Jerry told me that there was going to be a Mullins Family Reunion Dinner/Ball on December 19th and that I was invited. He told me told me that if I wanted to come all I had to do was call him up and the he would pay for my way to Illinois and back to Minnesota. I told Uncle Jerry that I'd call and let him know once I got back to Minnesota because I wasn't sure if I had to work or not on that day. But I knew deep down inside when I walked out of his house that I wouldn't be calling him nor would I be attending the Mullins Family Reunion Dinner/Ball. Why? Because I was no longer a Mullins anymore. I belonged to another family now. And plus I hadn't seen any of these people in seven plus years. Who was I to just show up at their family reunion?

As Sperm and I walked down the stairs he asked where we were parked. I showed him the car and he replied "I'll walk you to the end of the curb, but that's as far as I can go because I don't want this bracelet to go off cause then the cops we'll come. I gave Sperm a hug and he told me that he would send me a t-shirt as well as a copy of Donald's obituary, because Egg had stolen the copy that he pulled out earlier that night. I told him that I would send him copies of the picture that we had taken as soon as I got them developed. And I headed towards the car. As I walked towards the cars I saw Sperm give Egg a hug as well. I wondered, "How could Egg hate him so much? There has to be something that I don't know". I hopped into the back sit with Uncle John. Uncle John came with because he was going to be staying the night at Uncle Dollar's house. Within minutes Uncle Dollar and Egg got into the car as well and we drove off.

During the car ride back to Grandma Yolanda's house I asked Uncle Dollar if he'd give me a ride to the train station tomorrow morning and he told me that he would. My train was to leave at two in the afternoon so he told me that he'd pick me up a quarter to one. During the car ride Uncle

John seemed a little upset that I was holding a beer for Uncle Dollar until we got to Grandma Yolanda's house. Uncle John told me "You shouldn't be holding that beer for Dollar. Because then you'll get in trouble if we get pulled over. Plus you're too beautiful to be seen with a beer in your hand, if anything you should have a wine glass. But I am proud of you for not drinking tonight. I don't ever want to see you drinking". Within minutes we were a Grandma Yolanda's house when Uncle John stated "Dollar you got to let me go upstairs and see Yolanda, I haven't seen her in years"! So Uncle Dollar parked the car and we all headed upstairs. Once inside both Grandma Yolanda and Uncle John were excited to see each other. They joked around who was the skinniest between the two of them. And then Uncle John and Uncle Dollar left.

It was around nine thirty at night when I realized that I was supposed to hang out with Keith that afternoon. I called him up and apologized and told him that I had spent the entire day with my aunt and Sperm and that I hadn't seen them in seven years. Keith then told me that it was alright. I was at this point that Egg and Grandma Yolanda began to agree over Egg using the phone too much. Although Egg claimed that she was making toll free long distance calls, Grandma Yolanda still got upset. Why wouldn't she? Who's to say if Egg was even telling the truth anyway about the phone calls being toll free? So I walked in to the back bedroom so that I could hear Keith. I then asked him how his day in school went and he replied "My day went by extremely fast because I was looking forward to hanging out with you after school". I apologized again. Then Keith replied, "I wish that you weren't going back to Minnesota tomorrow". I jokingly replied "Well you're more than welcomed to come up and visit me anytime you want. I have my own place you know". "Maybe I'll come visit you on my spring break. But only if you come visit me first" stated Keith. And I told him "Okay, I'll come visit you". It was around this time that Egg came in to the room and told me that she needed to use my cell phone because Grandma Yolanda said that she was about to call the cops on her. So I told Keith that I'd talk to him later, and gave Egg my cell phone.

I walked out into the living room and sure enough Grandma Yolanda was on the phone calling the cops on Egg. It was at that exact time that someone rang the doorbell. It was Uncle Ernest James. I walked out the front door to go and meet him and tell him that he picked the wrong time to come over and that the cops were coming. But that didn't go as planned because he was so excited once he saw me. "Me-Me is that you? Come here girl and give me a hug! You're so grown up now and you talk just like a White girl"! stated Uncle Ernest James. I told him that now wasn't a good time because Grandma Yolanda had just called the cops on Egg. But he was convinced that he could patch things up. Once I walked back into the house I saw Egg packing her stuff. She told me that Uncle Dollar was on his way back over to pick her up. It was at this point that Uncle Ernest James began to ask them why they were acting all crazy and that they just needed to get along. Egg shouted, "Because I'm tried of everyone one treating me like I'm a mutherfucking child. I'm not about to let Yolanda or any other mutherfucker tell me what to do! I'm just not having it"! "Well Katherine, you know what you can do? You can get the fuck out my house because I'm not about to put up with this shit"! Replied Grandma Yolanda.

But Uncle Ernest James wasn't done yet. He was still convinced that he could solve the problem. This is when things got even worst. Grandma Yolanda stated "Ernest James you need to shut the hell up because you're not making anything better, and you can leave as well". Uncle Ernest James replied "I just came over here to see Katherine and Me-Me and here ya'll are acting a Goddamn fool. But fuck it I'll leave anyway"! "Get out. I don't have to deal with this shit"! Yelled Grandma Yolanda. But Uncle Ernest James still continued to talk and this made Grandma Yolanda even upset so she walked over to the telephone. "I'm calling the cops on your ass too"! Stated Grandma Yolanda. And she picked up the phone and called for another officer to come out to her house. It was at this point that I said "Grandma you know you can't keep calling the police like this all the time. Plus they both said that they'd leave".

I then helped Egg carry her belongings downstairs and as we were walking Egg said to me "It's a good thing that I'm leaving 'cause I'd been done hit that Bitch in her mutherfucking face. Disabled or not, I'm not about to have her telling me what to do". I could but at the exact same time I couldn't believe the words that had just came out of Egg's mouth.

I was shocked. The only thing that I could say was "Well if you actually thing that you become so mad that you'd hit her. Then for sure you're doing the right thing by leaving". I ran back upstairs and Uncle Ernest James was gone. I asked Grandma Yolanda were he had gone to and she told me "Girl he looked out the window and saw the cops pulling up, and he took off"! I looked out the window and sure enough the cops were outside. I told Grandma Yolanda that I would go downstairs and let them in. I ran downstairs and told the police officer what was going on and that everything was fine now. But I told him that Grandma Yolanda would still want to talk to him.

Once upstairs Grandma Yolanda thanked the police officers for coming out and told them that everything was alright now. So the police officers told us to have a good night and they left. Within minutes there was a knock at the door. It was Uncle Ernest James. He had come back to apologize. Uncle Ernest James stated "Mama's dead now. And this is the time when we're supposed to be coming together as a family. Not fighting with each other". I couldn't have summed it up any better myself. Uncle Ernest James was right and we all knew it. Grandma Yolanda sat in a her motorized wheelchair looking out the window then she turned and said "Well I'm tired. And I'm about to go to bed". Uncle Ernest James knew that was a hint for him to leave so he left and Grandma Yolanda and I went to bed.

Chapter 26
I Can't Stay Here Another Day

Wednesday, December 8, 2004 was the day that I was scheduled to return back to Minnesota. I woke up early that morning when Grandma Yolanda came in to the spare bedroom and told me that I had a phone call. I asked her who it was and she told me that it was Egg. I must admit that I was a tad bit pissed off that I had been woken up simply because Egg was on the phone. I answered the phone and it was Egg calling to tell me good-bye. She was also calling to tell me that she was going to be staying in Illinois until December 17th, and that she would be staying with Auntie Lola. She then told me that I should have Uncle Dollar bring me by Lola's house before I left so that she could say good-bye to me in person. That's when I told her "Look, I'm trying to go back home today and I'm not going to risk missing my train by going out of the way to stop by Lola's house just to so you can see me before I leave. Plus he's doing me a favor and I'm not about to have him driving all over town.

Once I got off the phone with Egg I went into Grandma Yolanda's room. I told her that Egg had just told me that she would be staying in town until December 17th. Grandma Yolanda responded, "What the hell is she staying here that long for"? I told her that I didn't know and I really didn't care. If was at this point that I also told Grandma Yolanda what Egg had said about her the night before. I told her "Grandma, My mom is going to be in town for nine more days and I'm leaving today. Last night she mentioned something to me about become angry with you and hitting you. So once I leave I don't want you to let her in your house under any circumstances. No matter what she says don't let her in. I checked the house and she took all of her stuff with her last night so there is no reason why you would even have to let her in. Because if I found out that my mom did anything to hurt you, I swear on my life that I would never speak to her again. I feel kind of bad leaving town when you guys are fighting like this but I have to go".

It was around eleven in the afternoon when my cousin Tommy and his older sister Nichelle stopped by. They were Uncle Ernest James eldest children. Tommy had brought his daughter Jessica and Nichelle had brought her daughter Princess. The four of us sat around and laughed about old times as Jessica and Princess played among themselves. I even pointed out how I remembered that Nichelle had done my hair for me the night before my fifth grade pictures. This I remembered mainly because it was the last picture I had taken of me before I moved to Minnesota. I then stated that that "This is my favorite school picture. I remember that you did my hair all pretty and pick me out a pretty outfit. This is something that my mom should have done. But she was too busy getting high". Nichelle then responded "Girl don't feel bad. Our daddy ain't no better. She also told me that he wasn't allowed in her house.

It was around this time that I brought up that I had seen her dad the night before. I stated "Yeah you dad stopped by last night at the wrong time. But he was really nice". Grandma Yolanda then filled both her and Tommy in on how she called the cops on both Egg and their dad the night before. Grandma Yvonne then mentioned how Uncle Ernest James had disappeared when the police came, but then mysterious reappeared once they left. Nichelle joking replied "He probably ran outside and hide in the trash can until they left". I laughed but at the same time I replied, "That's so mean". Then she replied, "What else am I supposed to say."? I laughed a little bit more and then I said "it's kind of funny that you guys feel the exact same way about your dad that I feel about my mom". So who was I to say that Nichelle was being mean by talking bad about her father? I was very much aware of the fact that I did the exact same thing when the topic of Egg was brought up. The only difference is that whenever I saw

Egg in person I still called her "Mom", as when they saw their father they called him by his first name. Although Mitchell and Jacob referred to Egg by her first name "Katherine". For some odd reason I couldn't do it. In a way I felt obligated to call her "Mom".

To my surprise Uncle Dollar picked me up at a quarter to one as planned. His girlfriend Ginger came with him as well. Neither one of them knew for sure how to get to the train station so he decided that he would stop by his friend mike's house because he was sure that Deion knew the way. Once at Deion's house, he agreed that he'd show us how to get to the train station after he was done frying some chicken. I looked over in the skillet and I was fully aware that Deion had just started frying the chicken. I sat downstairs in the basement with Uncle Dollar and Ginger and I remember saying "I'm going to be so pissed off if I miss my train". Uncle Dollar replied, "You want he's almost done frying the chicken". Then Ginger replied; "Now Johnny, you know damn well that he just started frying that chicken". From that moment on went sat in silence and waited for Deion to get down frying his chicken. It was around one forty-five when we left Deion's house. I had honestly believed that I would make it to the train station on time. That is until Deion said that we had to stop and get some gas first. It was at that point that I realized that there was no way in hell that I was going to catch the train that left at two ten in the afternoon. There was just no way.

We made it to the train station at two eleven and me, Uncle Dollar, and Ginger ran into the train station. They told me to run and that they would be right behind me with my suitcase. So off I ran, I ran to the front desk and asked the lady that was standing there if my train had left yet. She told me that if I ran that I could catch it because it was leaving in two minutes. The lady standing at the desk told me that I needed to go to gate B. I ran to gate B with Uncle Dollar and Ginger trailing behind me. But once I got there the doors were shut for both gate A and B. as I stood there very confused looking a gentlemen that worked for the train station asked me where I was going. I told him Minnesota and he replied, "You need to go to gate C". I ran in the direction that the gentlemen pointed. But once I got there I didn't see a gate C. I only saw gate E. it was at that time that I turned around to see that the exact same gentlemen was standing there.

He told me that I was too late and that the train had already left. And I was pissed. I knew that another day spent in Illinois would just make me angrier that I wouldn't be attending my grandmother's funeral.

I walked passed the front desk and the lady replied, "You missed your train huh". I replied, "Yes". I then asked her if there were any other trains that were leaving for Minnesota that day and she told me no. I then asked her if she knew of any bus companies that would be going to Minnesota. She gave me the phone numbers of local bus companies. I remember her saying to me "Can't you stay for another day? Your train ticket is good until June". That's when I shouted with tears in my eyes "I can't stay for another day, because I don't want to stay for another day. I need to get back to Minnesota right now"! Then I stormed out of the station. I walked out of the train station in silence with Uncle Dollar and Ginger once again trailing behind me. As I walked out of the train station I cracked a slight smile. This was due to the fact that I had remembered that seven years earlier I was the eleven-year-old girl that cried the entire bus ride to Minnesota because I didn't want to leave Illinois. Now almost eight years later her I was a nineteen year old girl about to start crying all over again. But this time it was because I wanted desperately to be in Minnesota, but I was stuck in Illinois.

After I missed my train, Uncle Dollar and his friend Deion decided that they'd make it up to me by buying me a pint of Gin. I guess I must have mention something to him about Gin being my drink of choice. I was then invited by all three of them to come over to Deion's house to eat some chicken and get drunk. But as much as I love chicken and getting drunk, I had to decline. I was still too pissed off. I told them to drop me off at Grandma Yolanda's and that I would call them later once I was ready to drink. I arrived back at Grandma Yolanda's house around three fifteen and went to bed. I woke up around six thirty and watch television with my grandma. Needless to say, I never called Uncle Dollar. I didn't want to get drunk with them anyway.

It was around eight thirty at night when I received a phone call from Sperm. He told me that he had a great time hanging out with me last night. He also told me that he was sorry that Uncle Dollar had made me miss my train. Sperm then told me that he had gone to court today and that he was no longer on house arrest anymore. He also added something about if being Egg's forty second birthday. I could've cared that it was Egg's Birthday. Plus, why should I? When just nine months earlier Egg called me well over a week after my birthday had passed. I'm more than positive that she was drunk when she left the message on my phone "I was just calling to wish you a happy belated birthday Baby Girl"! Plus if I called to wish Egg a happy birthday then she would know that I was still in town and I really didn't feel like being bothered with her. So needless to say, I didn't call.

As soon as I got done talking with Sperm he told me that Uncle John wanted to talk to me. I told Sperm to have a great night and then I began talking to Uncle John. The first words out of his mouth were "Timesha, you have no idea how mad I am that Dollar made you miss your train"! I told him that it was ok and that I would be catching the train tomorrow instead. He then mentioned that Uncle Dollar had told him that he bought me a pint of gin. Uncle John told me that he was once again proud of me for not drinking. He then told me that earlier that day after Uncle Dollar dropped me off that he had gotten so drunk that he left the interior lights on in the car. Uncle John said "The car is dead now. But I'll make sure that it gets jumped so that you don't miss your train tomorrow"! I told Uncle John that that was alright because I had already found another ride. I told him that my cousin Tommy would be giving me a ride to the train station instead. Uncle John replied "I don't blame you for finding another ride. I would have done the same thing".

I told Uncle John to have a great night as I had told Sperm. Then it was time for me to get some rest. Grandma Yolanda and I had a big day ahead of us tomorrow. So we thought.

Chapter 27
Home Sweet Home

Thursday, December 9, 2004, Grandma Yolanda and I both woke up at eight o'clock that morning. We had made plans the night before with Tommy. The three of us along with Jessica were to go shopping and buy clothes for Grandma Mrs. Rolland to wear at her funeral. Tommy had told us that he would be picking us up at nine o'clock that morning. It was a little after eleven when Egg called and said that her and Tommy were at the funeral home. I was pissed. Egg had gotten up earlier that morning and had thrown a monkey wrench in our plans. She had called up Tommy and had had him driving her around all that morning. Not to mention that fact that she was very inconsiderate to the fact that Grandma Yolanda and I had already made plane with him. But Egg didn't care. Instead she had Tommy drive her to the funeral home so that she could try and get more information. But when that didn't work she had him drive her over to Auntie Ellen's house.

To this day I still don't know what the reasoning was behind Egg calling us from the funeral home. Tommy soon called back and told us that he would be over to take me to the train station around a quarter to twelve. Grandma Yolanda and I were both preying that he would drop Egg off somewhere before he came to pick us up. Unfortunately, our preys weren't answered. Big surprise! So Egg showed up with Tommy and once agin Egg being the inconsiderate person that she is didn't even care that she had made Tommy three hours late for picking us up. Nor did she care that Tommy had a small two-door car and that he had Jessica's car seat in the back seat as well. As Grandma Yolanda and I walked down the stairs I noticed that Egg was sitting in the front seat. I became even more pissed. I said to Grandma Yolanda "Look at her sitting up there in the front sit. All I know is that I'm about to go crazy if she thinks that she's about to sit in that front seat. If anybody gets to sit in the front seat it should be you not her considering that fact that she shouldn't have even came with".

But there was no need for me to go crazy, Egg for once put someone before herself and let Grandma Yolanda have the front seat. I sat in the back seat of the car. It was at this point that I became extremely happy that Jessica had a car seat. This way I didn't have to sit right next to Egg. The entire car ride to the train station Egg kept trying to talk to me. But the only five words that she could get out of me were "I could honestly care less"! Egg tried telling me that Grandma Mrs. Rolland's funeral was going to be on Monday. I replied, "I could honestly care less"! She also told how she had gone out to Auntie Ellen's house and that Auntie Ellen started to cry once she saw her. Now this I could not see myself saying, "I could honestly care less" too. So I shouted "She cried when she saw you. That's funny! I bet she wasn't crying when SOMEONE was spending all of Grandma's money on shopping sprees and fur coats! I bet she wasn't crying when SOMEONE was taking trips to Las Vegas and throwing Hotel parties with Grandma's money"! The entire car was quiet. I shouted some more "I'd be crying too knowing that my mother was taken advantage of like that and now she was dead. Yep, SOMEONE spent all of Grandma's money and now we barely have enough money to bury her properly"! I ended the conversation by saying "I hope Auntie Ellen dies. I hope she dies and rots in hell for allowing Grandma to be taken advantage of like that. And I tell you one thing, that's one death that I wouldn't be making a trip back to Illinois for"!

There I said it. I let out all the anger that I had ha built up inside of me for the past four days. I said it. And I meant every single world that came out of me mouth. Because every single world that came out of my mouth came directly from my heart. The car was once again silent. To my surprise no one interrupted me while I was talking. Not even Egg. I knew that this was mainly because they were feeling the exact same way that I was. After I was done talking Egg replied, "Timesha, we've all done our wrong. But you shouldn't let hate consume you." I pretended as if I didn't even hear her talking to me. I sat there looking out the window thinking to myself "So now after all these years, Egg wants to preach to me about doing right. What kind of shit is that"! Egg than began to talk some more about how she had hung out with Nick (The guy that her and Grandma Yolanda fought over), and how he wanted to see me. I then went back to my "I could honestly care less" response. She also stated that if she had known that I had missed my train and that I was still in town that they would have stopped by. I sat there thinking to myself "Did it ever occur to her that the reason why I didn't call and tell her that I had missed my train was because I didn't want to be bothered by her"! But I'm more that certain that it never crossed her mind because Egg lives in an imaginary world that revolves around her and her only.

We arrived to the train station a little bit after twelve in the afternoon. Which was two hours before my train was scheduled to leave. But I didn't care, I figured that it better to be early than late as well as better to be safe than sorry which I had experienced first hand yesterday. Once we were at the train station Egg felt the need to walk me inside. I told her that she didn't have to and that I would be fine. But she insisted so I went along with it. I knew that in a matter or minutes I would no longer have to deal with her anymore. As we were walking down walking down the escalator, once again Egg tried talking to me about Grandma Mrs. Rolland's funeral. This is when I exploded on her. I stated, "Look I don't mean to sound like a Bitch, but I could honestly care less about anything that you are saying to me. And I don't care to discuss any of it"! Egg responded with "Okay". Once we were downstairs and I was on my way to gate B. Egg told me to have a safe trip and then asked for a hug and a kiss. I gave Egg a hug, but then I told her that I couldn't give her a kiss because "I don't want to smear my lipstick". Then I told her good-bye and walked away.

I then called my mom at work and told her that I would be home that night. I told her that Tommy had brought me to the train station extra early and that there was no way that I was missing my train again. My mom asked me if I knew anything else about my grandmother's funeral. I told her "Yeah, it's not going to be until Monday". She responded by saying "I'm sorry honey that you won't get to go to the funeral". I told her that I was upset but that I would be alright. I also replied "If I had just come back to Illinois a year earlier I could have seen both Uncle Donald and Grandma Mrs. Rolland. But now it's too late and I'll never see them again"! My mom told me "Honey things like this happen everyday. You can't blame yourself for returning back to Illinois when you did. You had no idea that your uncle and grandmother were going to pass away when they did". I knew deep down inside that my mom was right. But still felt somewhat guilty. I told my mom that I'd talk to her later once I got back home.

I didn't have anything else to do as I waited for the train so I worked on a little math homework. Time flew by quickly and the next thing I knew it was time for me to board my train. The train left the station at exactly two ten in the afternoon. I slept and ate potato chips the entire train ride home. I was extremely excited to return back to Minnesota due to the fact that I missed my family and friends. Although I was only gone four days, it seemed like I was gone for weeks.

I arrived back in Winona at seven forty eight at night on the same Amtrak train that had just pulled out from Chicago four and a half hours earlier. I knew that I had safely made it back home when I glanced out of the train window and saw my mom standing outside waiting for me. I noticed that she had a look of relief on her face once the train stopped. This look of relief was because she knew that she no longer had to worry because her daughter had found her way back home. Some people might say that I was doomed from the beginning, but as you can see, it's all nonsense.

Acknowledgments

First, I'd like to start off by addressing the two people who mean more to me than anyone else in this entire world, and that's my mom & dad! I'd like to apologize if I offended either one of you in anyway, shape, or form with any of the material that was written in my book. I also want both of you to know that you did the best you could've done when it came to raising me! I mean, let's face it, I was "Damaged goods when you guys received me"! I'm Joking! But on a more serious note, you were both college students and hadn't the slight clue as to how you should go about raising a fourteen year old! Plus anyone who knows both of you, would agree that if you guys would've got a hold of me when I was younger, this book wouldn't even exist! I Love You both because you did the one thing in May 1999 that everyone else refused to do, and that was take a "chance" on a kid that you knew nothing about! Now, here we are ten years later, and I want to Thank You both for taking that "chance" as well as giving me a "chance"! But most of all, I want to Thank You both for saving my life, because whether you realize it not, you truly did save my live! And I Thank You Both, I am forever in your Debt!!!

Next, I'd like to address my biological grandmother who is the one & only family member who has kept in contact with me throughout my entire life! Now, people can say what the want in regards to all the horrible things that she may have done to me when I was younger, but I look at it this way: if it hadn't been from my grandmother, myself nor my brothers would've had a place to live, food to eat, clothes on our bodies, or even a bed to sleep in when we were growing up in Illinois! You see, the one thing that many people fail to realize is that when the going got tough and everyone else kicked us out, my grandmother was always that one person who'd take us back in. And even though my grandmother physically wasn't able to care for herself, (due to the stroke that she suffered back in 1996 that left the entire right side of her body paralyzed) she still agreed to let me stay behind and live with her in Illinois. But I couldn't do it! I couldn't see myself taking the easy way out as well as moving forward in life without my brothers. But, as we all know, in less than two years, this is something that I would have to come to terms with. I Love You Grandma and I just want to Thank You for always being there throughout the past twenty-four years of my life, but even more so the last twelve years of my life because that's when I needed you the most! And I say that's when I needed you the most simply because you could've abandoned me like the rest of my biological family did, but you didn't! And I Thank You! You also didn't have to mail me countless gifts each year from Illinois to Minnesota for my birthday and Christmas, but you did! And I Thank You! Nor did you have to buy a train ticket and travel from Illinois by yourself spending a total of twelve hours between there and back, just to attend my High School graduation party, but you did! And I Thank You! I Love You Grandma and I am forever in your Debt!!!

To Amber Diekmann, also known as my one & only Best friend in the entire world! I just want to thank you for always being there for me anytime that I've ever needed you. You have been, and without a doubt in my mind, I know that you will always be that one and only person that I can talk to about anything without ever having the fear of being judged! Because, no matter what the situation was: I expressed how I felt, you said how you felt and no matter if you agreed with my final decision or not, you accepted it! And to me, that's what "Real" friends are supposed to do support your decisions even though sometimes they may not necessary agree with them! Thank You for accepting me for who I am and looking past many of the poor choices that you witnessed me making first hand! But most of all I want to Thank You for being my Best friend and being okay with it seeing that you & I both know that we have absolutely nothing in common! I'm Joking! But Thank You for all the support;

advice, comfort, loyalty, trust, and overall Thank You for giving me one of the best friendships I've ever had in my entire life! I Love You!!!

I'd also like to thank the rest of my Family, Friends, and Everyone who has given me all the support I could've asked for when it came to writing this book. I Love You All!

To the rest of you who don't agree with the book! I said it before and I'll say it again, I'm not proud of my past, but I'm not ashamed of it either. So, here I am: take me or leave me, I don't care! Everyone has a past and I can't undo what's already been done! I may not be perfect by any means, but giving the circumstances and the events that I've gone through in my life, I'd have to say that I turned out extremely well! I mean of course there were times where I wanted to give up and even a time when I just tried to end my life all together! But I'm still here which means that I must have a purpose of some sort in life! I'm a fighter, I always have been & I always will be! You've read the book, "I came, I saw, and I'm still here"! There's nothing you can do to me that hasn't already been done! Nor is there anything that you can say to me that hasn't already been said!